RE~~DIS~~CONNECTED

RE~~DIS~~CONNECTED

HOW 7 SCREEN-FREE WEEKS *with* MONKS *and* AMISH FARMERS HELPED ME RECOVER *the* LOST ART *of* BEING HUMAN

CARLOS WHITTAKER

NELSON
BOOKS

An Imprint of Thomas Nelson

Published in Nashville, Tennessee, by Nelson Books, an imprint of Thomas Nelson. Nelson Books and Thomas Nelson are registered trademarks of HarperCollins Christian Publishing, Inc.

Published in association with The Bindery Agency, www.TheBinderyAgency.com.

Thomas Nelson titles may be purchased in bulk for educational, business, fundraising, or sales promotional use. For information, please email SpecialMarkets@ThomasNelson.com.

Unless otherwise noted, Scripture quotations are taken from The Holy Bible, New International Version®, NIV®. Copyright © 1973, 1978, 1984, 2011 by Biblica, Inc.® Used by permission of Zondervan. All rights reserved worldwide. www.Zondervan.com. The "NIV" and "New International Version" are trademarks registered in the United States Patent and Trademark Office by Biblica, Inc.®

Scripture quotations marked ESV are taken from the ESV® Bible (The Holy Bible, English Standard Version®). Copyright © 2001 by Crossway, a publishing ministry of Good News Publishers. Used by permission. All rights reserved.

Scripture quotations marked NKJV are taken from the New King James Version®. Copyright © 1982 by Thomas Nelson. Used by permission. All rights reserved.

Emphasis in Scripture is added by the author.

Any internet addresses, phone numbers, or company or product information printed in this book are offered as a resource and are not intended in any way to be or to imply an endorsement by Thomas Nelson, nor does Thomas Nelson vouch for the existence, content, or services of these sites, phone numbers, companies, or products beyond the life of this book.

Library of Congress Cataloging-in-Publication Data

Names: Whittaker, Carlos, 1973- author.
Title: Reconnected : how 7 screen-free weeks with Monks and Amish farmers helped me recover the lost art of being human / Carlos Whittaker.
Description: Nashville : Thomas Nelson, 2024. | Includes bibliographical references. | Summary: "In the summer of 2022, podcaster and author Carlos Whittaker spent seven weeks entirely screen free, splitting his time between a monastery, an Amish farm, and home with his family. Blending the inspiring story of this experiment with practical guidance, Whittaker reveals how you can reset your relationship with screens and step into a life of real connection"-- Provided by publisher.
Identifiers: LCCN 2024013669 (print) | LCCN 2024013670 (ebook) | ISBN 9781400246465 (trade paperback) | ISBN 9781400246458 (ebook)
Subjects: LCSH: Self-actualization (Psychology)--Religious aspects--Christianity. | Distraction (Psychology)--Religious aspects--Christianity. | Internet--Social aspects. | Computer users--Attitudes.
Classification: LCC BV4598.2 .W557 2024 (print) | LCC BV4598.2 (ebook) | DDC 158.1--dc23/eng/20240520
LC record available at https://lccn.loc.gov/2024013669
LC ebook record available at https://lccn.loc.gov/2024013670

Printed in the United States of America

24 25 26 27 28 LBC 5 4 3 2 1

To the monks at Saint Andrew's Abbey
and to the Miller Family.
You changed everything about how I live,
and I will never tire of telling the world your stories.
Thank you for inviting me in.

CONTENTS

CONTENTS

INTRODUCTION

WELCOME TO THE EXPERIMENT

I t sounded like a great idea.

Everyone said it was a great idea.

It felt like a great idea.

Until I was standing digitally naked—phoneless, laptopless, iPadless—in a scorching-hot parking lot in the middle of the high desert of Southern California. It was a 101-degree day in late July, and I was staring after my best friend, Brian, as he drove away without a care in the world, leaving me to face the first of many challenging realizations I would have over the next seven weeks.

Namely, that no, this was *not* a great idea.

This was, in fact, the worst idea I had ever had.

I instinctively reached into my front left pocket to grab my phone. *Ugh.*

"Excuse me, Carlos?" said a voice behind me. I turned to see an elderly man wearing a simple brown robe. Father Patrick.

"The bells will ring five minutes before prayers are prayed and meals are served," he said. "Prayers will be in the chapel in front of you, and meals will be in the dining hall behind me." Father Patrick didn't really look me in the eye. He sort of looked past me and to the left as he was talking. Almost as if he didn't want to look deep into the soul of a conflicted man who had just entered what Father Patrick knew (but I did not) would simultaneously be the hardest yet most healing season of my life. The father pointed to a small cabin at the top of a nearby hill and said, "That's where you will be staying."

Saint Andrew's Abbey is a literal oasis in the desert. Although it's surrounded by rugged mountains filled with coyotes and cacti, the abbey itself is a lush retreat. Green lawns everywhere. Beautiful cottonwood trees providing shade from the scorching sun (so many cottonwoods!). Gardens, ponds, fountains. Like, it legit could be the perfect spa setting for the Southern California rich and famous. Just add some Wi-Fi, a masseuse, *and my phone*, and I would have been in actual heaven. Because although I was surrounded by twenty monks who probably felt like they were in heaven, I was having the complete opposite feeling.

"What have I done?" I whispered to myself as I followed Father Patrick on the six-minute hike up to my cabin overlooking the abbey.

What I had done was quite simple.

I had decided not to look at a single screen for the next seven weeks to see what screen time was doing to my head, hands, and heart. To see what had been missing. Part one of this experiment would involve hanging out with twenty Benedictine monks in the high desert of California for two weeks. For part two I would fly to Middle America to hang out with 125 Amish people in Mount Hope, Ohio, for two more weeks. And I would wrap up with three more screen-free weeks at home with my family.

That's right. Monks. Amish. Carlos. *Seven weeks without looking at a single screen.*

This whole dumb experiment began about a year ago with a single pop-up notification on my phone. The notification told me I had averaged seven hours and twenty-three minutes a day on my phone that week. I put my thumb on the notification and almost swiped up like I did every week when I saw it. But something stopped me this time.

I hovered my thumb over the notification and stared at it.

What does that mean? Seven hours and twenty-three minutes a day?

Something inside me wanted to do some math. I hate math. But I wanted to do this math. The math could quite possibly take me down a road I honestly didn't want to travel. The math was probably going to make me do something stupid. Looking at the math could actually ruin my career.

So I did the math.

When I clicked the notification, it took me to the Screen Time setting on my iPhone. *Here goes.* I opened my calculator and started entering numbers to see exactly how much of my daily human existence I spend staring at seven inches of LCD.

Okay, so I spend sevenish hours a day on my phone. (I'm counting the twenty-three minutes as *ish* so I don't have to do *that much math*.) I felt like that seemed normal. I mean, I make my living on my phone. I share my life and all our zany family adventures practically live for all the world to see. I try to write thoughtful posts on Instagram to help people navigate difficult conversations. It's okay. Seven hours a day is okay, right?

Right?

Then I started doing the real math.

Seven hours a day for seven days a week. What's that equal per week? The math told me I spend forty-nine hours every week looking at my phone? *Ugh.* Now the math feels gross. I don't even need a calculator to do that math. (Heather and I homeschooled our kids, so that's why I'm so math smart, in case you were wondering.)

Forty-nine hours is two full days out of each week. Not two workdays. No. That's two full twenty-four-hour cycles of life—two days in which a normal human being would wake up, eat, live, work, and then sleep for eight hours. Yeah, two of those days.

This wasn't a welcome realization. *Should I keep going with this math? Well, I've come this far . . .* Okay, so let's see. If I spend 49 hours on my phone each week, that means I spend 196 hours a month on my phone.

Eight days a month.

Eight full twenty-four-hour cycles of life.

That's also 2,352 hours a year.

Or a little less than one hundred days a year.

One hundred days a year! On my phone.

What in the world? I needed to do one more equation.

The average male in America lives until he's seventy-three years old. If I make it to age seventy-three (and thank God for that Whittaker DNA, because all my grandparents have made it that far), and if I continue to spend seven hours a day on my phone, I will spend nearly seven of my remaining twenty-five years of life creating and consuming content on a device.

There. Is. No. Way. We. Were. Created. For. This.

In a very real sense, we are more connected today than at any other time in human history. We get a constant stream of notifications about the latest updates from family, friends, and whatever social media influencers we follow. We're bombarded with a potent blend of news, celebrity gossip, and advertisements.

But somehow this hyperconnectivity feels an awful lot like *dis*connection.

I know we weren't made for so much screen time simply because we're more connected and more divided than we have ever been. Just the week before I did the math on my phone usage, I told my wife, Heather, that I didn't want to have dinner with this couple that we used to have dinner with all the time. The reason? I saw something one of them had reposted on social media that I thought was horrible. That post sent me down a rabbit trail of imagining what this couple must think about all these other issues I am passionate about.

That train of thought made me despise them for a moment. And suddenly I didn't want to spend time with fellow human beings I'd counted as friends—all because of something that I probably was never supposed to know in the first place.

Can you relate to that?

I mean, think about this: Do you think our souls and our psyches and our bodies were created to absorb the amount of information we now consume regularly? Like, every day? Are we really supposed to know the vast scope of what we can access? Are we supposed to know about all the devastation in every war-torn country? Are we supposed to know about the suffering in every corner of the globe? I'm not saying that the crises happening all over planet Earth are not important, but I am saying this: These phones have not just increased the volume of information available but also accelerated the speed at which our brains are filled with that information—and it seems to me that our souls aren't ready for that kind of barrage. We weren't designed for it.

What did humans do before we were so hyperconnected and distracted? How did we exist when we knew only what we were supposed to know about our friends and family? How much healthier were our minds when we didn't hold a phone in our hands for our work but instead worked the land with our hands? How much louder was God's voice when the volume of life was turned down low enough to hear him? Sometimes it seems like God is silent today, but maybe it's just that the volume of life has been so loud lately.

What have these phones and screens all around us done to our mental health—and our physical health as well? What have they done to our spiritual health?

If there's ever been anyone ideally positioned to investigate these questions and find out the answers, it's me. Mister Three-and-a-Half-Months-a-Year-Staring-at-His-Phone. I was scared that if I didn't do something drastic soon, maybe, just maybe I would miss the entire reason I was put on planet Earth.

So here's the idea as I pitched it to my literary agent, Alex, in an email back in 2021:

I'm going to go back to what I think we were designed to be and do as human beings. I know that there will never exist a future world in which we don't have technology connecting us in myriad ways. And to be honest—and I need to say this out loud—these devices and screens haven't been all bad. They've actually done so much good in the world too. I know firsthand the power of humans connecting through screens and changing others' lives. I've seen my Instagram community raise over $1 million for others in need over the past nine months alone. I know good can come from these screens. So the point of this experiment isn't going to be to burn the phones! No. Ultimately, I hope this experiment is going to help remind myself and others to "own the phones so they don't own us."

This was what I was going to do.

And this is what I did.

And this is what you're going to read about in this book.

"Alex, I'm going to go live as a monk. And then I'm going to live as an Amish farmer."

I hit Send on the email, and within a few hours I got a reply.

"Carlos, this is so needed. Great idea!"

My heart started to beat faster. *Am I really going to do this?* Ironically, the idea that I wouldn't be able to tell the world what I was learning in real time already felt suffocating. I normally spend my days digitally hanging out with my Instafamilia (the community that hangs out on my little corner of Instagram). Isn't that a trip? However, the reality was probably the other way around—I was suffocating right then and just didn't know it.

I should probably say a little something about my rationale for this experiment. Why hang out with monks and Amish farmers?

There's a simple beauty to the Benedictine monastic order of the Roman Catholic Church. Monks commit to three vows: stability, fidelity (to the monastic way of life), and obedience. Oh, to have a truly stable existence rooted in the qualities of remaining faithful and cultivating an obedient heart! I expected that a single day with these monks would wreck me in all the right ways. But fourteen days? *Lord, have mercy.*

So my head and my heart needed to be reset, and this reset would start in an environment of silence and calm at Saint Andrew's Abbey. But I knew my head and my heart weren't the only things that needed a reset.

What about my hands? My soft, uncalloused, LCD-screen-touching fingers were not created to be this clean. I believe our fingernails were probably created to have more dirt under them than they currently do in our modern, comfortable society. I believe we were created to touch the earth every day in ways most of us no longer do. I also believe our heads and hearts are deeply connected to our hands and how often we dig them into the earth. There are actual studies and data that support this.[1] What do we miss because of the shift in how we use (or don't use) our hands?

That's why I wanted to live with the Amish—because the Amish live technology-free and work the land with their hands. They live a devoutly religious life, and although I was certain that, as with the Catholic monks, I would have some real theological differences, I hoped fourteen days with my hands deep in their dirt might heal some as-yet-unidentified thing in me that needed healing.

Oh, and one more thing.

Before I launched into this experiment, I decided to add one more data point. I went to Los Angeles to get a complete workup from a neuroscientist—a brain specialist named Dr. Daniel Amen. He scanned my brain when I was at seven hours a day of screen time, and then he scanned my brain again two months later at zero minutes a day of screen time. I wanted to know if I could see what all this content consumption was doing to my brain. I had so many questions.

If there was damage from screen time, could it be healed?

Would there be a difference after two months?

What would surprise me?

What would I learn?

Most importantly, what would I change in my life going forward, and what would I bring back to the land of screens? Because if you're reading this, you know I didn't get rid of my screens permanently. I didn't type this book on a typewriter. I came back to the digital world full force. Or did I? I guess you're going to have to keep reading to find out.

Let me give you one more sneak peek into the story you are about to read. I thought this was going to be an experiment about screens and phones and me. But I was wrong. Because when I took the screens and phones away, it quickly became an experiment about me.

And I hope that as you read, you will begin to uncover the depths and beauty of the experiment called *you*.

PART 1

MONK SCHOOL

CHAPTER 1

IDENTITY

When I had arrived at Saint Andrew's a few hours earlier, I had FaceTimed my wife and kids one last time before Brian left with my phone. The kids were at camp and Heather was at home with her best friend. My last communication with them showcased them not really caring about my upcoming reality because they were surrounded by their favorite people in an alternate reality.

"I love you guys. Please pray," I said.

"We love you too, Dad!" the kids replied.

"You'll be fine," Heather lovingly chimed in.

Oh, the difference between their lot and mine.

Father Patrick looked like he could be brothers with Patrick Swayze and Gandalf. Yes, that's a thing. He was maybe seventy and shuffled a little faster than some of the other monks I saw walking around. As we walked up to what would be my home for the next two weeks, I stumbled through my first real conversation with a monk.

"So, how long you been a monk?"

Not a bad start, but then I followed up with, "What's your monk job? I mean, do you have jobs? Like, besides praying and stuff—I know *that's* your job. Not that you think it's a *job* or anything. I know you enjoy it, so it doesn't really feel like a job. Right?"

My first monk convo wasn't going well.

"I'm the retreat coordinator," Father Patrick said. "I handle all the guests coming to the abbey and try to make their stay as pleasant as possible. You are going to be staying at Mount Carmel. That's the one-room cabin. It's quite a hike up, but it's got a great view. And that way you can write your book with fewer distractions. That is why you are here, correct? You are writing a book?"

Notice he answered only one of my monk questions.

"Oh, well, actually, I'm here to do a sort of experiment—on myself," I replied. "You see, I spend about seven hours a day on my phone. That's almost a hundred days a year, and I wanted to see what life is like without screens. I decided to come to a monastery so I wasn't around phones and so I could just pray and stuff."

"We have phones," Father Patrick said, correcting my assumptions as he pulled his out of his pocket.

I was shook. *Monks have phones?*

"We aren't living in the 1800s, young man. Monks have phones too."

When we got to Mount Carmel, I was in love. This was literally the cutest, most perfect writer's cabin. It was sitting at the top of a desert hill. Behind it and to the south the hill continued to climb upward. Joshua trees and boulders littered the landscape, and there was a path pressed into the side of the hill.

Behind the hill, about ten miles away, I could see the outline of the San Gabriel Mountains standing guard over the desert. Directly in front of the cabin was the grounds of the monastery. I had a sweeping view of the tree line, the pathways, the pond, and all the green grass. Despite the desert climate that made most of the surrounding area brown and dry, the grass at Mount Carmel was a vibrant green thanks to sprinklers scattered around the property. Their distinctive tapping sound became a sort of rhythm to the place. *Tap-tap-tap-tap-tap*. And the blue sky. The vast Southern California desert sky. It was a dream.

We walked onto the porch and to the front door.

"The key is a little finicky," Father Patrick said. "You just have to wiggle it a little and eventually it will open up."

When we walked in, we were standing in the kitchen. There was a small kitchen table to the left, and on the wall behind it were the fridge, the sink, and a little window over the sink looking toward the mountains. The other wall had a stove, a microwave, and a Mr. Coffee machine that looked like it came directly from 1985. That was the entire kitchen. About five feet away from the kitchen were a couple of twin beds. And there was a little alcove with a small futon sofa facing out these large windows in the same direction as the porch view. The bathroom was through a door adjacent to the alcove.

That was it.

Father Patrick pulled a folded piece of paper from his pocket and handed it to me. It had the daily schedule on it.

6:00 a.m.	Vigils (first communal prayer of the day)
6:30–7:30 a.m.	*Lectio Divina* (literally "divine reading, the spiritual practice of reading Scripture meditatively)
7:30 a.m.	Lauds (morning prayer)
8:00 a.m.	Silent breakfast
8:30–11:00 a.m.	Class and study, or assigned work
12:00 p.m.	Conventual Mass
1:00 p.m.	Lunch

1:30–4:00 p.m.	Assigned work
4:00–5:00 p.m.	Study, rest, or exercise
5:00–5:30 p.m.	*Lectio Divina*
5:30 p.m.	Vespers (evening prayer)
6:00 p.m.	Silent dinner
7:30 p.m.	Compline (evening prayer)

I'm about to pray—a lot.

"Let me know if you have any questions," Father Patrick said as he turned, headed out the door, and started shuffling down the long stone staircase that led back to the main campus.

"Oh! I do have one question," I called out. "Air-conditioning? Where is it?"

"The cabin doesn't have AC," Father Patrick called back without stopping or turning around. "But it's got a swamp cooler. It works okay if it doesn't get above ninety. I'd recommend not being in there during the middle of the day."

No AC? In the middle of the desert? Lord, have mercy.

I closed the door and turned on the swamp cooler. It sounded like the space shuttle was taking off above me. I opened my backpack, pulled out my journal, sat at the kitchen table, and started writing.

DAY 1

What have I done? I'm sitting at the kitchen table, staring at the fridge, wondering one thing: Am I going to make it? Am I going to make it through the four weeks away from my family and seven total weeks away from my phone? I'm not going to know so much of what is happening on planet Earth. What will I miss?

I think the most important thing to remember from today is what happened on my flight as I logged off Instagram. I was already feeling weird. Like, anxiety-wise. But I don't think I realized it. As I was typing my goodbye post, I legit was feeling lightheaded. I mean, I didn't sleep well last night, so maybe that was it. But the second I hit Publish, telling the Instafamilia that I was logging off for a while, I straight up had a panic attack. Legit. I'm serious. Cotton mouth. Armpits soaking wet. The plane cabin felt like it was spinning. Like I had a physical reaction to telling the internet that I was going away.

What was that, Lord? Seriously? Can you reveal to me what happened? I haven't had a panic attack in at least five years. I felt bad for the man next to me because I kept getting up to pee. I had to move. Am I that addicted?

Brian picked me up from the airport and we went to In-N-Out for my last meal before I started eating monk food. It was delicious. Double-Double with chopped chilies and well-done fries. This will be my last meal on earth and first meal in heaven. I know it.

Wow, my hand hurts. Carlos is not used to writing with a pen.

We laughed a lot on the drive. And then when we pulled onto the abbey property, my adrenaline started to spike again. This was actually about to happen. *Lord, give me the strength.*

I'm scared of a lot. Not far from the top of my list is sleeping in this cabin all alone where serial killers can sneak in and out with no one noticing. But right below that on the list of scaries is this: I'm scared of my own thoughts. Not because they are evil or dark, but because I just can't stop them from racing. They are already racing. And I don't really have the ability to slow them down. I can't pick up my phone and numb my brain with TikTok. I have to just exist in my own head for the next fourteen days—in pretty close to twenty-three hours a day of silence. I don't think I can do it.

Let's just see if I can make it till tomorrow.

This sucks.

I know. I was the picture of confidence.

And you know what I started to realize in that moment? That most of the confidence I had was built on other people's opinions of me. And not even their opinion of me but their opinion of who I was curating myself to be on their phones. And what were they thinking about me in that moment?

Nothing.

Why would they think about me? I was gone. And there were 2.3 *billion* other people on Instagram who could fill their thoughts.

What was going to happen when the very thing that brought me confidence on a daily basis was taken away? I was about to find out. *Rapidly.*

I hope you see the conundrum I was in. And to be honest, the one you're in as well. We all are. Many of us have built our confidence and identity on our wit, wisdom, and woo. Or on our skill sets, savvy, and smarts. And of course, why wouldn't we? These are all God-given gifts. It's not like we aren't supposed to be proud of those things and use them for good. But we have to ask ourselves how much of who we think we *are* as human beings is actually based on what we *do*. We are no longer human beings. We are human doings.

I got up from the kitchen table and walked out the front door and onto the porch. Putting both hands on the banister, I looked out over the monastery and saw two monks in their identical brown robes, walking very slowly and intentionally around the pond. They were having a conversation. Probably about God or something. I saw a nun walking out of the guesthouse below me with a few folders.

Three monks down the hill and to the left walked out of their dormitory. They were all wearing the same brown robes with thick, black leather belts. While they wore identical outfits, *they* were not identical—each possessing their own wit, wisdom, and woo, their own skill sets, savvy, and smarts. But they definitely seemed more like human beings than human doings. Why was that? Maybe they dressed alike and lived in this manner on purpose? Of course they did this on purpose. They sacrificed their own glory for the glory of God. They used their unique abilities to make God known. Their focus was on something greater than themselves.

As mentioned earlier, Benedictine monks take a vow to three things: stability, obedience, and *conversatio morum*, a Latin expression that means something like "fidelity to monastic life."

A monk vows *stability* to that specific community. That is where they will live forever—with those men. They did not join some denomination of monks where they will transfer from here to there. No, they vowed to this land and these hallways. They will grow old here. They will die here. Stability to this community.

The vow of *obedience* is a commitment to listen openly to Holy Scripture and the Rule of Saint Benedict,[i] but also to the abbot (the elected head of the monastery) and all the monks. To listen does not necessarily mean to follow blindly, but it does require giving full attention to what is being said.

The vow of *conversatio morum*, or *fidelity*, encompasses many things: simplicity, celibacy, daily fixed-hour prayer, communal meals, sacred reading, and constantly dealing with the ups and downs of living in a small community.

So each monk still has their own personality and unique gift

---

i. The Rule of Saint Benedict was written in 530 CE by Benedict of Nursia, an Italian monk who founded twelve communities for monks. The Rule provides spiritual and practical guidelines for monks living in community under the leadership of an abbot.

set. They've simply found a way to exist in a community where their identity isn't about finding *me* as much as it is about finding *we*.

Now hear me out. I'm in no way saying that self-improvement and making yourself better isn't a good thing. But what if you were to suddenly lose your ability to do whatever it is that you are known for? It's worth considering a few questions.

What would happen?

Would you be content?

Would you be at peace?

And the biggest question I think we are all scared to answer: *Would you still be you?*

(Told you this journey wasn't about a phone. There are plenty of books and research on the addictive nature of a mobile phone. This isn't going to be another one.)

I wasn't even to the end of my first day at the monastery, and God was already hurling questions my way that I didn't want to answer.

Probably because I wasn't on my phone. LOL.

The wrestle in that moment was big. And it was going to get even bigger.

What is your identity being built upon?

Is it being a good parent?

Is it being a good leader?

Is it being a great conversationalist?

Is it being an amazing singer?

What is it? And what if whatever it is were to disappear? Because you know that one day your kids are going to talk about your parenting in therapy, right? The very people who follow your leadership will someday decide they want a different leader. People enjoy your conversations, but there will be someone who will woo them with better wordsmithing at some point.

Vocal cords aren't forever.

None of these things are great to be building identity on. But man, isn't it funny how phones have really shifted our perspective? Like, there is an actual camera facing your face all day every day, begging you to let the world know how great you are and show off the gifts you have been given.

Of course, it's all about *me*.

Why wouldn't it be? You have the ability to display all the things that make you a "me" all day, every day.

But I was about to enter a world where not a single person knew or cared who I was. They didn't care that I'd written four books. They didn't care that I had three hundred thousand Instagram followers.

I was going to have to do my next seven weeks the old-fashioned way.

Face-to-face.

Monk to monk.

Farmer to farmer.

The bell started to ring, and my stomach sent a knot up to the top of my throat. I felt like I was sixteen years old again and about to walk into a new school in a different country where I didn't know the language.

I opened the front door of my cabin, stepped out, and started walking down to my first day of monk school.

CHAPTER 2
PERSPECTIVE

One of the first things Dr. Amen said to me when we sat down to go over my first set of brain scans was, "Do you see this dent? That's not supposed to be there. And we were talking on the way in, that you played soccer in high school and college. And you hit your head—"

"With balls *so many times*," I said.

This was not what I thought he was going to start with. I thought he would ask how much time I spent on my phone, because the results of my brain scans most certainly and clearly showed brain damage from playing *Angry Birds* nonstop in 2010 and *Candy Crush* in 2012.

But that's not what Dr. Amen started with. He began with the fact that I had played competitive soccer.

"You see this indention at the front of your brain? This little dent right here?" He had turned away from me and was pointing at a spot on a large TV screen showcasing a 3D model of my brain. I don't know what I expected to see, but I was fascinated. It kinda looked like the surface of Mars. Lots of hills and valleys and crevices and maybe even a crater or two for good measure.

13

Dr. Amen continued. "Your brain is soft—about the consistency of soft butter, tofu, custard—somewhere between egg whites and Jell-O. And it's housed in a really hard skull that has multiple sharp, boney ridges. And probably when you were playing, they weren't wearing the headbands to lessen the impact, and soccer balls aren't light. And when they get wet, they put a lot of force on your brain and your neck. You don't want to have a valley here, so we really need to act."

I was blown away. *I have a dent in my brain.* I can now attribute every single bad decision I have made in life to that dent. Sweet.

I am a fan of Dr. Amen. That's how I ended up in his office—because I'm a fan. And how weird is it to be a fan of a doctor? But welcome to TikTok. I follow him on TikTok, and when I came up with this idea, I wanted some sort of doctor to help me with it all. I'd watched numerous videos he had filmed with celebrities, where he scanned their brains and then went over the results with them—from NBA players like Michael Porter to pop singers like Miley Cyrus and Justin Bieber to media moguls like the Kardashians.

When I sent Dr. Amen a DM, I never in a thousand years thought he would respond, much less agree to see me. But I decided to give it a shot. And to my surprise, the second I hit Send on the DM, I saw "seen" underneath my message. *He just saw my message!* And then the three little dot bubbles popped up, indicating he was typing back. "Absolutely, Carlos. Would love to set this up. Here's my email. Let's get my team to make this happen."

What's the saying about taking a shot? You will never hit your target unless you take a shot? No, that's not it. Maybe I'm making that up. Okay, either way, insert some Pinterest-worthy quote about taking a shot here, and let's all celebrate the fact that Dr. Amen *replied to me*!

I listened to him describe my brain as lumpy and communicate his desire to see it become less lumpy (but not totally smooth, because too smooth is bad but too lumpy is also not good). My thoughts immediately went to my dad. *How lumpy is his brain? How smooth is my brain? What did his brain look like in his late forties—when he was my age?* You see, my dad has dementia. Even typing that sentence doesn't seem real. The dementia has been progressing for years, and I still can't fully accept it. He has lost the ability to recognize who I am. Who my brother is. Who my mother is. It has been the cruelest of diseases to watch him battle. He was always a giant of a man as I was growing up and even after I became an adult. He could hold an audience captive with his words for an entire hour. He could deliver a message of hope with ease. Words were so easy for him, and now his mind has trapped him in a prison I'd never wish on anyone. So, as much as I wanted a baseline result on my brain scan, I was equally terrified of what Dr. Amen might find.

Before the brain scan I did about two hours of cognitive testing to assess how well my brain works. Feelings of anxiety shot straight to the top of my throat as the technician told me, "We are going to test your memory in a variety of ways, from remembering sequences of numbers to remembering faces to how quickly you react at seeing certain letters on a screen."

The technician walked me to a room and sat me down in front of a computer. The room was barren—very 1985 hospital vibes. I mean, I was looking left and right to see if Eleven from *Stranger Things* was going to appear in the hallway, coming out of a room where she was being experimented on. And the computer also gave an eighties vibe. The monitor looked like the one we had once attached to our Apple II Plus. I'm assuming they wanted the fewest distractions possible to get the most accurate results. Or the room designer really loved the eighties.

"The test should take you about an hour to complete," the technician said, and then he walked out and closed the door. There was a mouse to my right, and the cursor was blinking on the screen over the word "Begin." I didn't want to click it. I didn't want to begin a test that could tell me I was on the way toward a future filled with dementia. I didn't want the test to tell me that my memory was bad. To be honest, I was so terrified of what this test might reveal that I almost called it quits. I almost decided to walk out before I even took it. I didn't want to know.

Deep breath. Another, and then another.

I clicked Begin.

I spent an hour taking the test. One section asked me to remember groupings of numerals and then type them back into the computer. Another section spit out twenty words I was supposed to remember and then spit out forty words with some of the previously shown words mixed in. I had to click on the words I'd seen before and not click the new words.

Another section did the same thing with faces. It showed me forty small portraits in black and white. Then it displayed other faces mixed in with the first forty, and I had to click on only the faces from the original group. In the final section letters flashed up on the screen, and I had to press the spacebar every time a letter appeared *except* for the letter X. This was the most frustrating activity. I am freaking happy-trigger-finger Carlos. I'd never make it as a police officer. "Dang it!" I kept yelling every single time I screwed up. That was the only part of the test where I was shown how badly I was doing. All the other parts were being secretly scored somewhere I couldn't see. So when the test was finished, I was certain I was going to have the brain result of a Neanderthal.

Next they stuck me in a machine and scanned my brain for thirty minutes.

"I'm going to inject you with a liquid that will go to your brain and allow us to clearly see the SPECT scan," the technician explained. "It shouldn't have any side effects other than maybe a small headache later. But nothing bad."

I stuck out my arm without a second thought and let him jab it and inject whatever serum it was he told me about.

(Also, may I interrupt this story to tell you how terrifying it is that I will just let a random technician inject me with some liquid without even thinking twice? Okay, interruption over.)

"I know this is going to seem difficult," the technician continued, "but I promise you are going to be able to do it. It's all in your head." He chuckled before giving me the instructions for the next thirty minutes of my life. I wondered if he told that joke numerous times a day.

"You absolutely cannot move for any reason once we begin the test, okay? You have to hold your head completely still. I will tell you when you can move again. And you can't fall asleep. You need to be awake the entire time."

It would not be an exaggeration to say that the following thirty minutes felt like the longest thirty minutes of my life. The way I had to find a spot on the celling and stare at it for five minutes before finding another spot for five minutes and on and on. The way my nose *never tickles* until my hands are not allowed to touch my nose. After thirty minutes of mind games, the technician said, "Great job, Mr. Whittaker. You are all done." And of course, my nose stopped tickling the second he said that.

After the testing I met with Dr. Amen again. "So besides the lumps," I stammered, "did you see any . . ."

"You don't have a dementia brain, Carlos," Dr. Amen interjected as he looked me straight in the eyes. "I've seen many brains. You don't have one that's headed toward dementia. But there are also things you can do to keep your brain headed in the opposite direction."

Dr. Amen knew about my father's dementia from my paperwork. He proceeded to tell me all these things I could do to steer my brain toward health. He talked about what to put into my body and what not to put into it. He talked about important and really cool stuff, but all I could focus on was, "You don't have dementia brain." The breath I took after he said that was not a breath I was expecting. It was like I'd been holding my breath for hours and didn't even know it.

"Remember when I got off the elevator, I said 'I'm scared. I'm scared to look at my brain scans, scared to think about my dad's dementia.' But now I feel empowered because I'm thinking about those things instead of avoiding them," I said.

"What I find is when you do things to avoid your thoughts, they control you," Dr. Amen replied. "But when you actually face the patterns head-on, they dissipate. Sort of like a flashlight on a cockroach."

"Thank you, Dr. Amen," I said. "I absolutely will take your advice to heart."

We talked for another thirty minutes. We talked about my bouts with anxiety. We talked about my fear of sickness and how that had interfered in my life over the years. We talked about a lot, and he gave me great advice. But the statement that kept clicking in my head was that dementia did not have to be a part of my story. Just because my dad has dementia did not mean I will have dementia.

I had been gripped by absolute fear about my brain and whether it was headed the same direction as my dad's, and Dr. Amen set me free with eye-to-eye contact and only a few words. Isn't that amazing?

I had forgotten to put my phone on Do Not Disturb, so it had been buzzing insidiously the entire time I was in his office. But you know what I never did even one time? Pull out my phone to look at the notifications. Why? Because I was locked into this conversation, and nothing else in the world was more important to me. At that moment, literally nothing needed my attention more than this conversation with a doctor telling me what my brain looked like and how to avoid dementia. So although I felt those notifications and they were trying desperately to get my attention, they didn't get it. Because I didn't let them.

"I'll see you after your experiment, Carlos," Dr. Amen said. "Godspeed."

Godspeed. Yes, exactly.

He had no idea how prophetic that word would prove to be.

CHAPTER 3
GOD SPEED

The "no car" thing at the abbey was a situation.

There was no monk subway station either. I was going to have to use the two limbs attached to my torso at my hips. And although I really appreciated my cozy little cabin at the top of the hill, the word *hill* is in there. I was going to be walking the next two weeks—a lot.

I rushed out the door because I knew I had only five minutes to make it to the chapel for vespers, the evening prayer service. There are fifty-seven stone steps leading down from my cabin to the guesthouse, which sits at one end of the property's main road. The speed at which I ran down those steps was pretty incredible. I don't know what it is, but when there are that many steps in a row, the third grader in me rises up and I want to see how fast I can make it down the steps. I'll go even faster if someone is racing me. When I hit the bottom step, I smiled. As if I knew I would have beaten Heather or the kids on the way down.

I continued along a path in the middle of the lawn that led to the pond. The pond had a few ducks on it and lots of turtles around it just chillin'. I jogged past it and down the path to the chapel. The bell had rung at least four minutes earlier and I didn't want to be late, but the second I saw the chapel my heart started to pound. *What am I about to walk into? I'm not Catholic. I don't know all the rules. Am I going to make a fool of myself?* I took a deep breath and walked in.

The deep breath was a real thing, because I was kinda outta breath from hurrying down from Mount Carmel. The bell started ringing again, and I looked around to make sure that I was in the right place. "Where are the monks?" I wondered. I looked behind me through the floor-to-ceiling glass windows to see twenty monks lined up in two lines. Side by side. Looking straight ahead. *There they are! Here we go*, I thought.

Should I sit? Am I supposed to stand? There was only one other person in the chapel pews, and I made a decision to just do what he did. Legit, there was only one other person. This was the least attended church service I'd ever been to. He was sitting, so I sat down.

When the bells stopped he stood up; so did I.

The back door opened, and the monks began to chant behind us. The man began to chant as well. *Dang it! Was I supposed to study the chants before I got here? How does he know the chants?* And then I noticed he had a piece of paper in his hand. *Aha!* It was a chant cheat sheet. I scanned the chapel to see if there was a stack of them somewhere and finally spotted them on a table next to the door the monks were about to walk through. I made a beeline toward the back, but by the time I got there the monks were already starting to file in.

"Excuse me. Sorry," I said four or five times as I squeezed myself between multiple monks to reach the cheat sheet. They didn't look amused. I quickly grabbed it and dodged my way back through the monks to my seat.

Dodged is the right word. Kind of like when you are in the middle of worship at a charismatic church and you have to go to the restroom during the worship set. On the way back, you look around and everyone has their hands up and they are swaying side to side with their eyes closed. It's a game of inches as you dodge them to avoid getting accidentally worship-punched in the face on the way back to your seat. If you go to this sort of church, you know what I mean. You literally time your move to the beat of the songs, channeling Emmitt Smith hitting the hole in the line of scrimmage as if you're dipping and dodging defenders. That was what I looked like making my way back to my seat. I felt a bit smug when I made it without bumping into any of the monks. *I still got it!*

The distance between the back wall and my seat was probably only twenty feet, and although the round trip had taken me a good thirty seconds, the monks had made it only about halfway up the aisle—to where I was sitting. They were walking *slow*. And they were chanting *slow*.

I looked at the cheat sheet and started pretending like I knew what I was doing. I don't know who I thought I was trying to impress. Maybe the monks? Maybe the man in front of me who didn't even know I was there? Maybe myself? Maybe God? But I started chanting like I'd lived at the abbey for forty years.

The cheat sheet helped me about 0 percent.

The thirty-minute service felt like it lasted thirty years. Not gonna lie. Not gonna sugarcoat it. Not gonna make you think I was some Zen-loving, slowness-cherishing human at this point. No. This was monk school session one and I was *bored*.

We sat down. Stood up. Sat down. Stood up. Sang. Bowed. Sang. Sat down. Sang. Chanted. Repeated. Stood up. Over and over.

They sang *so slowly*. They read so *slowly*.

About as slowly as they walked.

When the service was over, I was starving. All of that standing and sitting and chanting really took it out of me. So I walked over to the dining hall to wait for the dinner bell to ring. I was the first in line. Once again, I found myself waiting for the monks. I turned around and saw them slowly making their way to the dining hall. Their rhythmic walking made their robes sway like bells on their bodies. Almost moving in sync with the others' robes. Some had their hands clasped behind their backs. Smiling at each other. Chatting quietly. I saw a few monks even chuckling. That's when it hit me.

I wasn't moving at the right speed. The speed at which I was moving was the speed of my regular life—which was *not* the speed at which life happened here. No. This was monk speed. Maybe we can even call it God speed.[i]

Back in the 1970s, a Japanese theologian named Kosuke Koyama wrote a book called *Three Mile an Hour God*. In it, he draws out the idea that maybe the speed at which God moves is the speed at which he designed us to move. You see, a human being walks at three miles an hour. That is our average pace. Now, some of you with longer femurs than mine will walk a bit faster, others a bit slower.[ii]

Koyama points out that Jesus' entire ministry was conducted at three miles an hour. He walked everywhere. His disciples walked with him everywhere. Nowhere does the Bible say that Jesus and his disciples had a pack of stallions they rode at a gallop around the

---

i. I know, I know. *Godspeed* doesn't really refer to God's rate of movement (or anyone's speed the way we usually think of that word), but stick with me here. This is wordplay that's making a point!

ii. Actually, studies show that from your twenties to your late forties, your walking speed increases, and women walk faster than men! This has nothing to do with Mr. Koyama's book—I just thought that was wild. Ladies, where are you going so fast?!

Holy Land. (Is a group of horses called a pack? Why does this feel wrong?)

They didn't have fancy two-story chariots that they rode around in. No. They walked. Everywhere. Probably around three miles per hour.

And if Jesus is God—which you actually don't have to believe for this to make sense, but if you believe as I do—then you can easily say that three miles an hour is God speed. Koyama goes on to write that love has a speed. And that speed is slow. And that speed is gentle.

This goes counter to how *so many* God followers live and even "do ministry." It flies in the face of God followers who think God is only interested in us being more efficient, faster, more productive. It makes you think that maybe this God we are all trying to figure out—this God who makes the earth spin and float, this God who threw the stars into the skies and breathed air into our lungs—did everything he did slowly and with intention.

This countercultural way of looking at God will actually mess you up in a big way. I mean, as I look at my own life, I think of the speed at which I produce content. I think of the speed at which I make videos that help people. I think of the speed at which I walk, drive, fly. Now, what I'm about to say isn't based on some theological concept, so don't try and exegete this because it's simply a thought that I'm starting to find helpful. If I say that I'm a follower of Jesus . . .

and I'm moving at one hundred miles per hour,
and Jesus is moving at three miles per hour,
then who is following who?

We often say that life is speeding us by. I'd beg to differ and suggest that maybe it's we who are speeding life by.

So what do we do? How do we slow down and start moving at God speed? Is the answer to buy a horse and buggy? Is the answer to stop flying? Is the answer to travel only as far as our legs will take us? Of course not. But we should think about the things that speed up our lives as we reassess our speed against God speed.

Here are a few things I realized in just the first few days of living and walking with the monks.

1. **WALK. MORE.** Seriously. If you are like 90 percent of people I know, you probably drive or ride or fly everywhere you go. There isn't a need for walking like there used to be. Five hundred years ago, most of us had to walk to get from point A to point B. That's no longer the case. So why do we need to walk? Well, to be reminded that this is actually *how* we were created to move. Beyond the *obvious* and *documented* health benefits of walking, some of us just need to be reminded that slow is good. That slow can be better than fast.

   I recently started walking around my neighborhood every single morning. The same streets that I drive every day. There is a home a few doors down from mine with a beautiful rose garden. I say *garden* because it's not just one bush. It is a bunch of manicured bushes I'd never noticed before. (Because I was going too fast.) And the noticing of the garden isn't what I want to sit on here, though I will get to that in the next chapter. No. It was the smell. The *scent*. Oh my goodness, I love walking past the roses, because I can smell them literally thirty feet before I get to them. I have driven by these same roses for years, even with my windows down. But have I ever smelled them? Not once. Why? Because I was moving too fast. This helped me understand the statement "stop and smell the roses" in an entirely new way.

2. **WALK. TOGETHER. MORE**. One of the places my family loves to vacation is New York City. Now, I know what you might be thinking: *What in the world does New York City have to do with living and moving at God speed? If ever there were a city that is the opposite of God speed, it's New York City.* Well, actually, that's not true. You can definitely live at God speed in a city. It's not like Jesus and his disciples just walked country roads. They were in bustling towns and cities all the time.

One of the reasons I love being in New York City with my family is that we have to walk everywhere together. And if you are walking in the city, you know what you *can't* be doing? Staring at your phone. Because if you do that you will end up either flattened on the street or running into scaffolding. That's right. It's dangerous to walk while looking at your phone. So that's why we have always loved going to New York City as a family. It's like an automatic screen-free day. It slows us down even in the midst of such speed.

3. **WALK. WITHOUT. TECH**. Sometimes it's okay to go on a walk without a fitness goal in mind. Without a place to get to. Without a podcast to listen to. Without a playlist to motivate you. Just walk because that's what you were designed to do. Ditch the Apple Watch and your phone. Trust me—your walk will count even if you don't know how many steps you've taken or how far you've walked. It will count even if you don't post a photo of you walking for the world to see. I walked for weeks at the abbey, and nobody that follows me on social media knew!

Just walk with you and you alone. The crazy thing is that it's actually *really* hard to do. You don't realize how alone you will feel until you ditch the tech on your walks. But when you do take that first tech-free walk, I promise you'll realize something else that I mean when I say it's hard to do. For example, there are some sounds you might not be used to. The sound of your own breathing. The sound of your feet hitting the pavement. The sound of *everything* around you that you didn't know was there because of those things that normally stick out of your ears.

So yeah, it might be different at first, but it is *so healthy* to walk without listening to or watching something on a device. I'm not saying that we've got to always walk without tech. I love walking or running to music. I'm just saying that I think it's important to also incorporate walks that look more like walks used to look. Back before we could multitask.

Just. Walk.

The monks finally made it to the dining hall. Hungry had now turned into *hangry*. I was fake smiling as they all walked past me to their tables. I followed the one non-monk man to a table separate from the monks. We awkwardly smiled at each other as we waited for one of the monks to pray for the meal. Surprisingly, I was anticipating getting to know this man sitting across the table from me. It was surprising because I'm something of an introvert and I like eating alone. But man, I'd been alone all day. I hadn't really said much of anything to anyone other than my conversation with Father Patrick.

I pulled the paper schedule from my pocket to see how long dinner was. It didn't say, just that it started at 6:00 p.m. But then I looked again and there was another word I hadn't noticed in front of *dinner*.

Silent.

Uh-oh. I was going to have to eat in silence after an entire after-noon of silence? And do so sitting directly across from a stranger at a table that seats twelve. *Why did I choose this seat?* Awkward Monastery Moment #4,232 already. Let's just go ahead and name these things AMMs. Or how about A-Double-Ems. That's got some flow to it. And it needs to flow because the number of A-Double-Ems I was about to experience over the next two weeks could fill an encyclopedia.

When the monk finally finished praying, I piled my plate with a mountain of spaghetti. And it was with the first slurp of a noodle that I quickly realized how loud I was when I ate. I glanced at my new silent friend with a look that said, "I'm sorry I sound like this when I eat." That's a look I've never given anyone ever. And I con-tinued trying not to eat loudly throughout what may have been the most awkward meal I'd ever had.

As I walked out of the dining room and headed back to my cabin, I said out loud to myself, "I don't think I can do this." I already missed my family. I missed my friends. I missed my dogs. But do you know what was wild? I didn't miss my phone. Not yet at least.

I walked back up to Mount Carmel a lot slower than I'd walked down. If I was going to be away from my family and life for a month, I wasn't going to waste it. But to be honest, I was struggling. "God, part of me knows this is going to be a good thing . . . but right now? Right now I don't want to do this. I don't want to be here. I want to go home." I prayed these words as I walked back up the hill, and I cried the whole way up. I was surprised by my sudden emotion and lack of confidence in this journey. I felt overwhelmed by the time I got to the cabin—like full-on overwhelmed. Almost sobbing.

I sat at the kitchen table and wrote in my journal:

I can't.

I got up and started to pack my bags. I'd made a decision. I couldn't do this. I was going home in the morning. Back to my family. Back to my life.

Bags packed. Me sobbing. I lay down and waited for morning to come.

CHAPTER 4

NOTICE

When I opened my eyes, it was pitch-black outside. I didn't know what time it was or how long I had been asleep. I didn't even know what time I had fallen asleep. I reached for my phone to see what time it was.

Joke's on me.

Then I grabbed the clock I had purchased at Target before I left Nashville. The clock didn't light up, so I still couldn't see what time it was. Joke's still on me. *Even the simplest things aren't simple anymore.*

So I just lay there. Alone with my thoughts.

Do I really need to do this? Is this a waste of time? Would anybody actually care to read the tormented thoughts of a man in his late forties who is addicted to his phone and what may or may not change if he goes without it for a while?

I mean, there are *plenty* of books already out there on the benefits of rest. There are plenty of books out there that tell us to slow down, plenty that tell us how bad phones are for our mental health. Did there really need to be another one?

And to be honest, there was *no way* I was going to become some digital minimalist. I *love* technology. I *love* screens. I'm the last person to tell anyone to put away their phones and stop documenting their lives. Having my phone in my hands and documenting my life *actually pays my bills.*

And I enjoy it. Of course there needs to be a balance. But this experiment wasn't about finding balance. Because balance for me is going to look different than balance for you. And nobody needs me to torture myself for nearly two months just to come back and say, "Find some balance." No.

This experiment needed to be about something else. Something more. I just didn't know what. And I didn't need to hang out at a monastery for two weeks and then an Amish farm for another two weeks if I didn't know what this was about. And at that moment, I surely didn't know what or why.

So I got up and tripped over the packed suitcase I'd put right next to my bed for some reason. When I say tripped, I mean full on, eighty-five-year-old-with-no-balance-in-the-dark tripped. Fortunately I caught myself on the kitchen table. Remember, the cabin's all one room. (Imagine a tiny studio apartment in Manhattan. Except take out the Manhattan part and add some really big bugs.)

I flipped on the kitchen light and looked at the clock: 4:33 a.m. Morning vigils wasn't until 6:00 a.m. I figured I'd just stay awake. I walked over to the ancient Mr. Coffee machine, spooned four heaping tablespoons of Dunkin' Donuts breakfast blend into the filter, filled the reservoir with water, and turned it on.

I sat down at the table and opened my journal.

DAY 2

God? I put a question mark next to your name because I am honestly not sure if you are listening. Reason being, I'd swear you told me that this was the right choice. That leaving my family for a month to enter into the monastic life and then the Amish life was going to help me help others. That I was going to find out why we should be off our phones. That I was going to help people with boundaries when it came to our phones.

But, God, this doesn't even feel like it's about phones anymore. Like, I am already over that part. I don't even want my phone back. I just want my family back. I just want my friends back. I just want to be around people that love me. I just want to go back and be a better friend. A better husband. A better human.

I don't need to disappear for a month to figure that out. So I'm going home. I'm going home to figure out what this whole thing is about before I spend any more time out here purposeless. I promise when I figure out the reason, I'll come back. But right now I don't have a reason. Right now I think I'm supposed to go home. So I'm sorry. I just don't know why I'm here.

And with that, it was over. After morning vigils I was going to call Brian to come pick me up and tell Heather I'd be coming home for now. Until I knew *why* I was here.

The Mr. Coffee started gurgling.

The sun started rising.

I grabbed my coffee and walked out the door to the front porch.

The sunrise was exquisite. Since the cabin was perched at the top of the highest point on the monastery grounds, I got a bird's-eye view of the entire abbey coming alive. First I noticed the squirrels. They were repeatedly spiraling up and down the gigantic pine tree to my right. Then they sprinted across the path and onto another tree before leaping back to the ground to begin their entire ritual all over again. They even traded who was chasing who. *Are they playing? What purpose does their little game of chase serve?*

The next thing I noticed were the ducks. I was about fifty yards uphill from the pond, and all at the same time they started squawking. Or I guess quacking. Who needs roosters when you have abbey ducks? But after a minute, I noticed that it was just one duck doing all the quacking. I wondered if that was annoying to his duck friends. I have a friend like that too.

I noticed a family of quail down at the bottom of the hill. They were marching in line across some rocks. *Are quail that hang out together a family or a flock?*

I noticed how the sun, which was rising from behind the cabin, gently and slowly illuminated one tree at a time.

I noticed a few monks walking out of their dormitories. Coffee mugs in hand, they were gliding at the same pace I'd seen them glide the day before. It was now 5:45 a.m. They were probably heading to the chapel for morning vigils.

And one more thing I noticed on my quiet little front-porch hang: My coffee tasted exquisite. Legitimately incredible. I do love a simple cup of Dunkin' Donuts breakfast blend, but I also know what a good cup brewed in a Chemex tastes like. And it doesn't taste like Dunkin' Donuts breakfast blend. But this pot? It's almost like a barista from Crema (my favorite coffee shop in Nashville) snuck into my kitchen, made a pour-over for me, and snuck it into the 1985 Mr. Coffee. *This coffee tastes incredible. Why in the world does it taste so good? This is weird.*

I finished the best cup of coffee I had ever tasted and began my trek down to the chapel.

After vigils, I headed to the phone in the retreat center office to call Heather. We had scheduled certain times that I would call so we could catch up on life. This was our first appointment and, unfortunately for my experiment, it was going to be our last. Because I was going home.

Four rings and then voice mail.

My greatest fear was being realized. The fear that my wife was in fact *not* sitting next to her phone just staring at it and waiting for my phone call.

I called back. She answered.

"Hey, babe! How is it?" she said. I could hear that she wasn't at home and was doing something else at the same time she was talking to me. I needed her undivided attention.

"I'm doing bad. Really bad, babe. Is this a good time? I need to talk to you. Seriously, I can call back later if it's better."

"Actually, I'm pretty busy the rest of the day. This may be my only chance to talk."

"Babe, I'm coming home. I can't do this. I don't know why I'm here. I wanna come home. I don't need to be away for weeks and weeks to figure out that we need to be off our phones more. I get it. I'm coming home."

"Have you asked God if you should come home?"

This. This was why I should not have called. Because Heather *never* gives in to my Eeyore pity parties, nor does she ever give me the advice I want. It's not that she doesn't have opinions about the situations I find myself in. It's more that she knows the advice I need isn't from her. It's from God.

"You wrote a book called *Enter Wild*, remember? You taught people how to have conversational intimacy with God. You should go read it."

Now she was trying to be funny.

"Carlos, you can do this. But I'm not going to stop you from coming home. I think you are looking at this the wrong way. You aren't there to learn how to have a better relationship with your phone. You are there to remember what it was like to have relationships with yourself, others, and God *before* the phone. And then to help us get back to that—while we still have our phones. Go talk to God. I love you."

This was not the conversation I wanted to have.

I hung up the phone, which was connected to a wall, and left the office. I started walking toward the front of the campus, as if I could just walk through the desert to LAX. I wasn't heading anywhere in particular; I just started walking. Morning lauds wasn't for another hour. *I'll just walk.*

I kept mentally repeating what Heather had said. *I'm not here to learn how to have a better relationship with my phone. I'm here to remember what it's like to have a relationship with myself, others, and God before we had these phones.*

And then it hit me. I had a lesson from my morning already. Something I had done numerous times already without realizing it.

I noticed.

Noticed.

Noticing is something we have a hard time doing these days. And not just because we are staring at our screens all day. I mean, sure, that is a major reason. But it's also hard because even when we are not staring at them, they are constantly buzzing and reminding us that we need to look at them, even when they are in our pocket.

So we don't notice.

I'd already noticed so much this morning.

The squirrels. The ducks. The quail. The sunrise. The monks and their coffee. *My coffee.*

I realized that it's not that my coffee tasted any better than when I am at home. It was simply because, since I wasn't reading my email *while* I was drinking my coffee, I was able to *notice* the flavor in a way I hadn't in so long.

This is why that first cup of coffee on vacation tastes so much better than the cup of coffee you drink as you are racing out the door in the morning on the way to work. Because you are in a space where you *can notice.*

———

Have you ever thought about the fact that most of us notice things *way* less than we used to? Let's not just focus on screen time. How about how the screens interrupt us from noticing? They keep us from noticing two very important and necessary things: the beauty and the brokenness of the world around us. And both are vital aspects of being human.

We need to be noticing both.

I noticed an incredible amount of beauty on my front-porch hang. I didn't necessarily notice any brokenness. But oh, how important it is for us to notice those around us who are hurting.

This is one thing that Jesus did so well.

He *noticed.*

Probably because he was doing two of the things I'd already been reminded of in the previous twenty-four hours: He walked at three miles an hour, and he took time to notice those who needed to be noticed.

He noticed the woman at the well.

He noticed that she was thirsty for more than just water—she was thirsty for love and acceptance. And he gave her both.

He noticed the tax collector, Zacchaeus, who was completely despised by his own community (and for good reason). But Jesus noticed the good inside Zacchaeus and his longing for forgiveness. Once again, Jesus gave what was needed.

He noticed the woman who was caught in adultery and filled

with fear and shame as she was about to be stoned. But because he noticed her, *he* offered her grace and mercy.

He noticed the lepers who were outcasts from society. He noticed their pain and isolation and offered them healing and acceptance.

Jesus' ability to notice people was central to his calling.

In my book *How to Human*, I spend a lot of time talking about the intrinsic need every human has to be seen. When we *see* someone, we can then *free* someone. But what I love about the difference between seeing and noticing is that it's possible to see someone without noticing them. To notice someone requires an extra step—that you have your gaze up! To notice a person gets you one step closer to freeing them. This is true because noticing happens *after* you see them. Beyond that initial moment of simply seeing, what do you *notice* about who they are and what they believe that can help you go deeper?

Do you want to know something I do that has helped me to become a way better noticer? It involves a phone. (See? These things aren't all bad.) I downloaded an app on my phone that reminds me to stop and notice. It reminds me three times a day at *random*. Yup. That's the kicker. The app sends me a push notification that simply says, "Notice." And this is what I do when it pops up.

I stop whatever I'm doing and take time to notice something I've never noticed before. Then I capture that thing with a photo or I write it down. What's great about this is that even if I find myself in the same place every single day doing the same thing, it forces me to stop and find something new. And after a while I started doing this everywhere even without the notification.

Let me give you a real-time example. I'm currently writing this chapter from the sofa in my living room.[i] And if the app sent me a

---

i. I know. This is exactly the sort of vibe location you imagine when you think of where authors write their books. Well, alas, this is mine.

notification right now, my first thought would probably be, *I've sat here for millions of hours of my life. There is no way I will see something I have never noticed before.*

But I would be wrong. Because I see my son's shoes under the side table to my left. And one of his shoes is tipped over so I can see the sole of the shoe. And I just noticed that the design on the sole has a sort of topographical map on it. Let me go see what it's a map of.

Okay, after closer inspection I discovered that the map is of a mountainous region somewhere. I guess I'll never know. But what I do know is that I would love to find out if there is a story behind it. I mean, of course there is. So when I'm done here, I'm going to do a little research to find out why the map is on the shoe. It's probably something the designer put there knowing that not many people will notice. So I *can't wait* to find out why it's there. I'm also going to take a photo and put it in an idea bucket I have so that if and when I am brainstorming and need an idea that involves a topographical map, maybe this will spark something.

Just think about all the incredible things that we don't notice around us on a daily basis. When it's time to go to bed after a long day, we plop down on our beds and grab our screens to unwind. But you know what happens when we do that? We don't notice the mattress beneath us. We don't notice how the comforter comforts us. C'mon, it's called a *comforter*! Legitimately, it's called that because it's supposed to provide us comfort. Have you ever thought about that? And what do we use as a comforter instead? Our phones!

Try this tonight. When you are ready for bed, walk up to it, pull back the sheets (this works way better if you *make your bed*), and when you lie down, pull the blankets over you and just lie there for sixty seconds. Notice the weight of the comforter on top of you. Notice the way your body sinks into the mattress. Notice the way your limbs slowly begin to relax. Once you have done that for a minute, then go ahead and grab your book or phone (although I recommend that you start leaving your phone in another room before bed, but we will get to that later) and do your pre-sleep routine. But notice the beauty of what is about to happen. Sleep is coming. And to notice that it's on its way is pretty wild.

Back to my desert walk.

About forty minutes into my nature hike, it hit me. I didn't have to ask God if I needed to leave anymore. Heather had answered that for me.

Now my prayer was simple: *God, help me notice all the ways in which we've forgotten how to be human since these screens have become attached to our palms. Show me the beauty of my human experience as I live disconnected for the next several weeks. Surprise me with lessons. Surprise me with you. Amen.*

I felt a legit shot of adrenaline and new breath in my lungs. I had a new way of looking at what I was about to experience. I was filled with anticipation.

While making my way back to the chapel, I purposely walked slower. I'd already learned that lesson. So as I leisurely strolled toward the chapel, I tried to take in as much as I could of the beauty around me and notice every single thing. The wind. The trees. The leaves. The grass. The sounds. I wanted to take it all in.

The bell rang. Lauds was about to begin. I made it to the chapel with two minutes to spare. This time I was the only one in there. My friend was gone. I grabbed the chant cheat sheet before the monks filed in. It was only day two and I was basically a professional monk already.

Bring on the lauds, I said to myself. *Bring on the freaking lauds.*

CHAPTER 5
WONDER

For the second time that day the monks filed into the chapel two by two, and it was only 7:30 a.m. And they had done it last night at 5:30 p.m. and 7:30 p.m. And they would pray again at noon. And before every meal. And they do this seven days a week, 365 days a year.

We were halfway through lauds when I grabbed a pen out of my sling pack and started scribbling on the back of the chant cheat sheet. My simple math, which was probably off a digit here or there, told me that these monks pray the hourly equivalent of *at least* forty-five days a year. As in forty-five full twenty-four-hour days. That's a total of three hours of scheduled prayer a day. And that was only the prayer I knew of, only what I was invited to as a rookie wannabe monk.

My mind was going a million miles an hour as to why. *Why this much prayer?* You know what I wanted to do? I wanted to look it up. I wanted to google it and find out why. Like, right then.

But I couldn't—and it was driving me crazy. I had to settle for wondering. I had to wonder and keep wondering without stopping my wondering. This was a *really* frustrating experience, if I'm being honest. Because for the first time in a long time, I could not scratch the itch. I could not scratch the wondering itch so I could stop wondering.

You do realize that is what it feels like now, right? How many times are you in a conversation where somebody wonders something only to stop their wondering in about three seconds flat because they can look it up on their phone?

We. Don't. Wonder. Anymore.

And because we don't wonder anymore, you know what else we've lost?

Wonder. As in the *awe-and-wonder* type of wonder.

<hr>

Let's rewind back to 1990, if you don't mind. I was walking down the aisle at Tower Records with my best friend, Peter, when I saw her. She was staring at me from across the aisle. I stared back. Hoping she was real. Wondering where she had been my whole life. Peter had continued on without knowing that this random girl and I had stumbled upon each other in the pop aisle and were having a moment. Staring probably a bit longer than would be socially acceptable. And it would have been the most romantic moment ever if it had two things attached to it:

1. If maybe, at the exact moment we locked eyes, Bette Midler's "The Wind Beneath My Wings" came on the speakers overhead. That would have locked in the moment for the both of us.
2. If she had been an actual 3D human staring deep into my eyes and not a life-size photo of Mariah Carey on her self-titled debut album.

But she was staring into my soul. "Peter! Come here!" I yelled. "Have you ever heard of her?"

"Nah, man. I don't listen to that stuff. She's *fine*, though," he said as he walked off again. I went over to the display and put on the demo headphones. I hit the plastic button that started spinning the CD.

Slayed. It was *over.* I had found my future spouse. (Insert present-day Carlos thanking God for unanswered prayers.) I picked up her CD, walked to the front counter, and bought the album that I would play nonstop for the next year of my life—all the while looking at her looking back at me from the cover and pretending she was singing to me alone.

"So who is this?" I asked the worker at the counter. The only thing they could tell me was that Mariah Carey was from New York. I raced home and turned on MTV. I waited for hours, having to suffer through Depeche Mode and INXS videos until *her* video finally came on. I had the VCR set and missed only the first four seconds of it. And then I had a video of my newest crush, Mariah Carey.

I wondered about her life every day for weeks. Not in a stalker way—relax—but more in a "Just who is she?" way. I learned all I could through listening to her lyrics, but there was no way to gather any sort of information back then besides waiting for the media to tell us. It was either going to be some friend at school who heard something first, or I would get lucky and stumble upon a broadcast interview while it was airing live on *Yo! MTV Raps.* Well, lucky for me, it only took a month and finally *Entertainment Tonight* was going to release a ten-minute interview with her. I set the VCR again. And I waited and wondered again.

Can. You. Literally. Imagine?

Can you imagine having to wait for anything like we had to wait back then? But this chapter isn't about the lost art of waiting.

It's about the lost art of wondering.

Waiting is what makes space for wondering to happen.

———

We don't have to wonder about much anymore. And when we do, it's often in anticipation of something bad, right? Like wondering what the doctors are going to say. Like wondering if he or she will say yes. Like wondering if we will get the job. And for many of us, that wondering leads to anxiety. I honestly think it's because we don't know how to wonder anymore.

Just because we don't know something, it isn't the end of the world. What if we aren't *supposed* to know everything we do know? I honestly believe that is the case. When was the last time you wondered for something that kept you wondering for weeks? Hardly anything makes us wonder like that anymore. And here I found myself wondering about something I knew I could find the answer to in a matter of seconds if it had been forty-eight hours earlier when I had my phone. But now I would have to wonder for a lot longer than a few seconds. And it was driving me crazy. Oh. And if you forgot what I was wondering about . . .

The word *wonder* has a few different definitions. As a verb it's used like this: "to think or speculate curiously. . . . to be filled with admiration, amazement, or awe; marvel."[1]

And I think I'm actually talking about both of these. You see, the first definition leads to the second. Right?

Curiosity leads to amazement. But nowadays, there seems to be much less time between the first and the second definition. To speculate. *That was all we did in the nineties.* And I think the length of time between speculation and amazement is what we need to get back to. Listen, I don't want to get *super* deep on this, but I wonder

(See what I did there?) if by losing our sense of wonder, we lose one of the biggest parts of our humanity. When we lose our sense of wonder and our ability to wonder, do we also lose the connection to ourselves, others, and the world around us?

I see two big dangers when it comes to losing the ability to wonder.

The first is simple: *we lose the ability to not know.* Have you noticed that one of the phrases we hear less and less is "I don't know"? The phrase "I don't know" has almost become obsolete. And the reason why? Because we can find out almost anything we need to know within seconds of wondering about it. But that's just the beginning of the problem. The continuation of the problem is that now we feel like we *must* know everything. That we must know everything about the geopolitical issues of our day. That we must know everything about our bodies and physical sciences. That we must know everything about God and everything that God represents and is.

And the truth is that we *can't.* We can't possibly know all of this. But we *feel* like we need to. Which leads to all sorts of problems, and perhaps none bigger than this: If we can't admit that we don't know something, suddenly we are creating experts who aren't actually experts. Suddenly, watching three hours of TikTok videos on the latest global humanitarian crisis makes us an expert, and we stop wondering and start declaring. Oh, that we would realize that this is *so* not human. We were created to wonder! We were created to *not* know!

The second danger when we lose our ability to wonder is that *we lose so much creativity.* Creativity is the way in which we see the world and its problems in new ways. When we lose creativity, we lose the ability to come up with new solutions to old problems. So we fall back into old patterns of behavior and thinking, which inevitably leads to a loss of vitality in life! Can you feel my fingers begin to type all of this at a much more rapid pace? *Wonder is wonderful!* And we've lost the ability to do it—the ability to wonder and our sense of wonder.

These are two things I believe are *essential* to our existence as humans. So how do we get them back?

1. **DON'T RUIN YOUR WONDER BY ALWAYS FINDING THE ANSWER**. I know this is a hard one, but try it for a week. When you have a question about something, just let the question live in you for a while. Let it simmer. Because the questions themselves often lead to more self-discovery. Questions lead to questions. It's all a part of our design. When you quickly find the answer to something, you are no longer engaged with a part of your brain that used to be engaged much longer.

2. **KEEP LEARNING**. Like, legitimately. What is something you can learn right now? Something you're a complete rookie at? Every year on January 1, I make a decision to become a rookie at something new. Nine out of ten times, I fail miserably and never get past the beginner stage. I've done magic, knife making, drone piloting, break dancing, fly-fishing, and so much more. Out of all those things, the one thing I kept doing was fly-fishing. Because it's the one I'll never conquer. I'll *always* have to wonder what the fish are eating and how to present the fly to them so that they get tricked into eating it.

   And then when I finally land the big one, I'm filled with *awe* and *wonder* as to how majestic this fish is. Then I release it to go tell its brothers and sisters to come play. And this was something I started in my forties. I didn't grow up fishing. Nope. I decided later in life to let it fill me with wonder. And now I *wonder* about fishing all the time and it fills me with *wonder.* It's become a part of who I am.

So let's call a spade a spade here. These screens we hold in our hands have severely limited, if not completely destroyed, our ability to wonder. Which has reduced the amount of awe and wonder in our lives. And that is a really horrible thing. What is more human than gasping at something that fills you with wonder? All because you wondered about it in the first place? (And can I just say that the longer we have to wonder about something, the more of a gasp we will let out when we finally get the answer.)

Wonder no longer comes naturally. Like me sitting in the chapel pew while the monks were praying. It wasn't natural for me to just wonder about it. But I had to wait. And wait I did.

Following the prayer time, I quickly exited the chapel and started trailing the first monk I saw.[i]

The closer I got, the weirder it felt to be mall walking toward a monk. I say *mall walking* because I'm assuming that is what I looked like trying to catch up with him while trying to not run. I wasn't looking to get kicked out of monk school so quickly.

"Um, excuse me. Brother? Father? Hi. I have a question," I said.

The monk turned toward me a lot slower than it took me to even catch up with him. "Yes? What is it?"

"I was wondering. Why so much prayer? What does it do for you to pray so much? I'm just learning about all you do. Could you answer that for me?"

"Oh, why yes," he said. "You see, we believe that everything we do is prayer. We live a life of prayer. There is something you must read that can explain it much better than I can. There is a pamphlet

---

i. Trailing = chasing.

in the used bookstore—I think it is in the back room on the second shelf. It will give you a much clearer picture than I could. It's a letter from Saint Jerome from the year AD 385. Come find me after you read it, and we can talk about it."

With that, the monk slowly turned around and began shuffling back to his dormitory. I wanted to ask his name, but for some reason it felt like I was just supposed to let him go without interrupting his prayer shuffle once again.

Back of the bookstore, Saint Jerome, AD 385, I kept repeating as I hurried to the bookstore. It was about a three-minute walk, and when I got to the front door and reached to open it, I saw that the light inside was off.

I cupped my hands around my eyes and pressed my face against the glass to see if I could get a better look inside. Maybe there was a monk in there who was meditating or something. I squinted and stared. Nope. It was empty.

On the other side of this door was a pamphlet that would allow me to scratch the wonder itch. When I twisted the doorknob, it kind of halfway turned. *Is it breaking and entering if the door is unlocked but the lights are off?* Obviously, I wasn't actually breaking into the monastery bookstore, but it did feel like I was in secret-agent mode.

When I walked in, it smelled exactly like you might imagine a used bookstore at a monastery would smell. I couldn't find the light switch, so I just let my eyes adjust to the dark and started walking toward the back room. The ceiling was super low, and there were books everywhere. Not only on the shelves but also piled inside boxes.

By the time I got to the back room, my eyes had adjusted enough to see. I scanned the books, looking for the pamphlet. It was exactly where the monk had said it would be: *Wisdom from Saint Jerome*.

I picked it up and walked back out to the front room where all the morning light was pouring through the large windows. There was a chair that didn't look like anyone had sat in it for a few years, so I sat down and opened the pamphlet. I didn't know who Saint Jerome was, but I did know he was about to help me find the answer I'd been looking for during the last sixty minutes. It felt like an eternity.

And then there it was.

The Apostle indeed admonishes us to pray without ceasing (1 Thessalonians 5:17), and with the Saints their very sleep should be a prayer. Nevertheless, we must set aside stated hours for the duty of praying. Then, should any occupation keep us away from it, the hour itself will remind us of that duty. As such prayer times everyone knows of the third, sixth and ninth hours, the morning and the evening hours. Nor should you ever take nourishment without beginning to do so with a prayer. Likewise, you should not leave the table without discharging your duty of thanks to the Creator. In the night, too, one should rise from his couch two or three times and therewith recall what he has learned by heart from the Scriptures [during the daytime]. On leaving his abode he should arm himself with prayer. Also, he should say a prayer upon his return before he seats himself again. After that only is the life entitled to its nourishment and the body to its rest. Before every action, at the beginning of every undertaking, let the hand make the sign of the cross.[2]

Wow. So that's it. That whole "pray without ceasing" part—they *really* take that literally. That made sense, but now I had more questions. *Do some monks pray even more than these monks? Do they get bored? Do they pray the same things over and over?* Suddenly, my wondering turned into more wondering.

I kept reading the pamphlet.

Apparently, we should strive to pray at *all* times, but just to make sure we're at least pulling it off with some consistency, the church came up with "canonical" or "fixed hours" to pray: morning, evening, and nighttime, as well as prayer at the third, sixth, and ninth hours (9:00 a.m., 12:00 p.m., 3:00 p.m.) called Terce, Sext, and None.

As overwhelming as this might seem, especially for an unstructured, creative, fly-by-the-seat-of-his-pants guy like me, I'd already prayed more in the last day than I had in weeks. Plus in twenty-four hours I'd managed to have a nervous breakdown, overcome said breakdown, spend less than ten minutes actually talking to another human being, pray for a total of two hours and thirty minutes with a bunch of monks, and sneak into a monastery bookstore. All in twenty-four hours. I was monking.

I opened my journal to start processing all that I had figured out when I had a quick thought: *There doesn't have to be a lesson in everything. Sometimes just* being *is the lesson.*

I had a lot of days left of this experiment, so I needed to slow down all this realizing and just do a little more being. *You've got time to figure this all out, Carlos. Just take it in and let it pour over you.*

So I shut my journal, took a deep breath, stood up, and left the scene of the crime. I decided not to write anything in my journal for a few days. I was just going to be.

CHAPTER 6
BEING

spent the next few days trying to just *be*. As an author, Instagrammer, and content creator, I am constantly trying to squeeze a lesson out of every single thing I experience. To be clear, it's not something I consider a bother; I love doing this. It's fun for me to help people by unpacking my own experiences. But I was trying not to overanalyze every interaction. Because truth be told, sometimes life is just meant to be lived.

Sometimes a sunset is just meant to be seen. To be enjoyed without capturing and sharing it.

Sometimes a good meal is just meant to be eaten and enjoyed. Not to be analyzed and improved. Not to be documented and posted.

It's funny how even without my phone, my journal was kind of becoming my phone. The first few days, I reached for it at every opportunity to document a thought or a feeling or an insight. And then I had a realization: Maybe it's not the *phone* that's the problem with us not living like we used to. Maybe it's the idea that we need to keep improving our lives. And in the midst of all of this self-improvement, we miss the beauty and simplicity of life as it is right in front of us.

Speaking of beauty and simplicity, let me take you into the beauty and simplicity of a typical tech-free day at the abbey. Every day there seemed designed to draw me into what I was actually created for: simply *being*.

———

My day begins the night before when I put four heaping tablespoons of Dunkin' Donuts breakfast blend into the Mr. Coffee and set the brew time to 4:50 a.m. I no longer need an alarm clock because I quickly trained myself to wake up to nothing but the gurgling sounds and heavenly aroma coming from the Mr. Coffee eight feet away from my pillow.

After rolling out of bed and shuffling over to the Mr. Coffee, I pour a piping-hot eight ounces into the Waffle House mug I brought from home. You know the mug I'm talking about if you have ever been to a Waffle House. This mug is hefty, thick, and the lip is curved just enough that it almost feels like you are kissing it. (I know. That's way too sultry of a way to describe a mug, but if you know, you know.) Greatest mug on the planet.

I take my mug and shuffle out to the front porch to just sit and watch the grounds come alive with every inch of sunlight as it rises over the tree line. The first cup of coffee is my bird-watching cup. The second cup is my prayer cup. I pray until it's gone. I pray for my wife, my kids, my friends, and myself. Sometimes I taste some salt that my eyeballs accidentally deposited into my cup.

I start heading down to the chapel around 5:45 a.m. for 6:00 a.m. morning vigils. I really love this service. It's my favorite prayer time of the day with the monks because I enjoy watching them stumble in looking just as sleepy as I am. One of the brothers always has the hardest time keeping his eyes open; his head bobs as he kind of tries to stay awake. I don't know why this makes me laugh so much. But it is the same monk every morning, and I think it is hilarious. Even monks have trouble staying awake and praying sometimes.

At 6:30 a.m., I start my morning hike. There is a cemetery at the top of the hill behind the main grounds of the abbey. It is about a twenty-minute hike, and the morning sky is always breathtaking. I know *cemetery* and *breathtaking* don't normally hang out together, but this place is incredibly beautiful in a desert kind of way.

I time it so I can hike up to the cemetery, spend time exploring, and make it back down by 7:30 a.m. for lauds. An important detail to insert here is that my father-in-law is buried there. He was an oblate at the monastery. What's an oblate, you may ask? They can be laypersons or clergy, men or women, who are not monks but seek God in association with a monastery to enrich their lives.

> With the *Rule of Benedict* as their guide, oblates engage in practices that are part of the very fabric of Christian spirituality, such as daily prayer and reflection and offering hospitality where they live and work. Christians of all faith denominations may become oblates and may be married or single.
>
> Oblates' lives are shaped by living the wisdom of Christ as interpreted by Saint Benedict. The word "oblate" means "offering," and they offer themselves to God in the service of others. Through prayer, service and community, oblates bear witness to the teachings of Jesus as seen through the lens of St. Benedict.[1]

Basically, my father-in-law tried his best to follow the monks' way of living without actually living here. Unfortunately, I never met him—he died two years before I met Heather. But he is buried up here next to all these monks.

I park myself right next to his headstone and we have one of our *talks*. Well, I guess I talk to him more than he talks to me. I tell him things I think he would have loved to know about Heather and who she is now. I tell him about the grandkids he never met. I tell him about me and how the more I learn of him, the more I see bits of me in his story. This part of my day has become more cathartic than I anticipated. I'm so grateful for these chats.

Lauds at 7:30 a.m. is way more caffeinated than 6:00 a.m. vigils. There is a pep to the monks' step and the songs are a bit sprightlier.

Breakfast is the first time I have any sort of close interaction with another human. I say "close interaction" because breakfast happens in complete silence, minus the sounds of forks scraping the plates and my own chewing and swallowing. But I'm not interacting with the monks. You see, the monks sit at the monk tables along the edge of the dining hall. There's also a head table for the abbot (boss monk) and a few others. The center tables are reserved for guests.

The abbey welcomes new guests all the time. Normally they stay for two days max. I am a blip on the radar of the abbey's normality. And so every morning I meet the guests who checked in the day before. When they walk into the dining hall, I see the same look on their faces that I had on mine the first time I walked in. The look that says, "Holy crap, what am I supposed to do? I don't want to mess anything up."

Although there are probably six large tables for guests, each seating about twelve, guests are asked to sit together. Imagine meeting someone for the first time with nothing more than a smile and a nod, and then having to eat in complete silence twelve inches away from them—all without the help of a screen you could use to avoid the awkwardness of the situation. The meal is filled with a lot of staring at eggs, and then glancing up to make sure you are not being rude, only to find yourself staring at someone right as they take a huge bite of something, and making eye contact only to immediately look away.

Breakfast is about forty-five minutes of silence, and then everyone heads out to their respective jobs and meetings. All the monks have jobs. Some work in the bookstore. Some work in the ceramics building. Some work in the guesthouses. Some work as professors. I normally head from breakfast back up to my cabin while it's still cool enough to be inside. (Remember, no AC in late July in the middle of the California desert.) I spend time reading my Bible and journaling my conversation with God. Then around 10:00 a.m., I head down to the lawn next to the dormitories, where there are a few apple trees. The trees are just big enough to provide some shade. The desert sun is no joke, but with the dryness of the air, the shade can make a ninety-eight-degree day feel like seventy-eight degrees.

I sit under these trees and talk to God. Out loud. I'm sure I look crazy, but it's good for me. Talking out loud to an invisible God is sometimes the only way I can feel like he is real. No journaling yet. Just talking. I am doing my best to just *be*.

After thirty minutes or so under the tree, the bookstore opens. In addition to the used bookstore, the abbey also has a regular bookstore. They both smell like you might imagine a monastery bookstore would. The regular bookstore is huge and beautiful. There is a lobby area with a gigantic fireplace and three large leather sofas surrounding it. I peruse the shelves for about fifteen minutes before landing on a book and heading over to one of the sofas to read for an hour or two. I quickly become friends with the bookstore staff, Maria and Glenda. They give me a few days of meandering around and smiling at them before asking the question almost every person living or working at the monastery has asked: "So why are you here so long?"

I give them my ninety-second elevator pitch about the experiment I am doing on myself, and then we have a longer conversation about their struggles with the phone and how they have a love-hate relationship with it.

Which is the truth, right? Even you, right now, I bet you wish you were on your phone less. I think 100 percent of us wish this because these screens have become such a necessary staple in our days. I'm gonna help you with this soon. I promise.

I leave my comfy spot on the couch when Maria and Glenda politely remind me that the bookstore is going to close until after noon mass. Remember, I don't have a watch, so I rely on bells ringing or reminders from friendly bookstore workers to be where I need to be.[i]

After mass we have lunch, and *we can talk*! The monks also sit with guests during lunch. This is when introvert Carlos *explodes* into extrovert Carlos. I say *introvert* because I think I am one. But the desire I have for connection with other people while living at Saint Andrew's Abbey is mind-blowing. I begin to think maybe it isn't that I enjoy being alone that makes me an introvert. Maybe because I spend so much time on my phone, I have a false sense of connection with a lot of people. Because without my phone, guess what? I'm still introverted, but it feels like a much healthier version. I still get my energy from alone time, but I'm enjoying this extrovert that I normally don't see in myself. I am actively looking for connection and interaction with people.

What if our ability to distract ourselves from face-to-face community by numbing our minds for hours on end with a screen *isn't* evidence of our desire to be alone? What if we have tricked ourselves into thinking we don't need to be with others as much as we actually do? Now, I'm not saying that there's no such thing as

---

i. Mass *was constantly a mess.* I tell you, the number of times I screwed up in mass was astonishing. If there were an Olympic sport for getting the stank eye from a monk, I would be a gold medalist.

a true introvert. I do believe some people are wired this way. But maybe, just maybe, I'm using a screen to mask my need for relational connection. Maybe I'm a pretend introvert, and all of you true introverts are judging me so hard for pretending to be one of you.

Ugh. Sorry, I wasn't planning to go so deep; I just wanted to tell you what a day of *being* at the abbey is like. But alas, no day at this monastery is without a lesson.

I meet so many wonderful people at lunch, some of whom I hit it off with and we end up hiking together or even reading books together by the pond.[ii]

After lunch I try to find a monk to spend time with. Again, you wouldn't imagine it but monks *be busy.* I quickly realize I have to get on their schedule if I want any time.

There is one monk specifically that I want time with. He is the former abbot of the monastery and is now retired from that role, but he still feels like the grand wizard of the place. Father Francis. I remember him from when Heather and I were dating, and we would come up to the monastery. He is a tall, jovial, whimsical man. When I ask if I can grab thirty minutes with him, he responds, "I may have thirty minutes on Saturday. I could squeeze you in." It was Tuesday. *Dang, Father. What in the world are you going to be doing?* I don't say what I'm thinking, but I do say, "Oh wow! Okay, that's great. Pencil me in!"

"I'm so sorry it can't be sooner, Carlos," Father Francis says. "It's a very busy week for me. I'm teaching two retreats back-to-back all day every day on healing from trauma, and then I have a few pastors from Los Angeles coming up for counsel, as I'm their spiritual director. I am also hosting the archbishop of Poland, who is flying in this weekend. I have a wedding to perform, and then I'm heading to Florida for a few days."

---

ii. Introvert Carlos is officially retired. Until I need to be alone again. LOL.

My mind is blown. This guy is busier than me back in my regular life. And he's going to *Florida*? The reality of this monk gig is expanding before my very eyes.

I spend the first part of the afternoon deep in the one nonfiction book I allowed myself to bring. I didn't want to bring a lot of books because I didn't want to replace my newfound freedom from one thing that consumed all my time for another thing that, if used incorrectly, could also consume all my time.

Then I spend an hour or two just walking. I walk around the grounds, noticing bumblebees or the way the winds blow. I walk the Stations of the Cross,[iii] watching out for rattlesnakes and bobcats as I go. A monastery walk feels much more adventurous when I think about both Jesus and bobcats.

I slowly make my way through the late afternoon until vespers at 5:30 p.m. The sun begins to set and I again find myself in the chapel with the monks, chanting our thanks to God for another great day of walking with him. These songs and prayers *feel* like they belong in the early evening. I love them.

Dinner is again taken in silence, although I do make sounds of glory and joy every time I shovel another bite of enchilada into my pie hole. The food is good! I am for sure gonna gain some pounds while I'm here.

From dinner I make my way to the pond and hang out with my duck and turtle friends until 7:10 p.m. This is my favorite time of the day. It's when I get to call Heather. Our quick check-ins are normally filled with me crying and her smiling. I can almost hear her smile on the other end of the line. She is listening to me shift and change

iii. The Stations of the Cross are a series of fourteen images depicting the events of Jesus' last day on earth. At Catholic churches and monasteries the images are typically arranged along a path so people can walk and pray from one image to the next as an act of devotion.

and heal. We try to talk every day, but some days she is busy and it doesn't work. At first my feelings are hurt when she can chat for only a minute, but then I remember she is alone at home running Whittaker Enterprises while I am walking around all day making friends with turtles and ducks. I call her from different phones on campus. There is even a pay phone booth. Like, a real-life, working pay phone. I love standing inside of it. I feel so 1985.

After a brief chat with my wife, I head back to the chapel for compline at 7:30 p.m. We pray psalms of protection, asking God to protect us in the night and from bad dreams and such. Then I leave the chapel and head back up to the cabin to watch the sunset. After spending about an hour on the porch, I move inside to the sofa and open up one of my novels. (It's like Netflix but a book.) And then I go to bed around 9:30 p.m.

This is the scaffolding of my days. And it is inside this scaffolding—filled with prayers, priests, and promises—that something really interesting begins to happen. Something I wasn't planning on. It turns out that this focus on just *being* led me to some important places.

My belief in God, which was evidently propped up by a lot of stuff I no longer had around me—begins to crumble a bit. This is happening because, by simply being, I'm suddenly able to see things in my mind and heart that I was too distracted to see before. After spending a lifetime gaining insights into my faith, I feel like God is beginning to ask me if I trust everything I've learned. That is a really frightening question to be asked when you are all alone at the beginning of a seven-week journey.

I don't know the answer to God's question, but if my belief is about to crumble, it may as well crumble right here—in the company of men who have dedicated their entire lives to trusting what they've learned. This new way of living is bringing a lot to the surface. And I'm not saying that's a bad thing. When we do more being, God may show up and interrupt our long-held beliefs. The simplicity of life at the abbey has brought me to a place of wrestling.

I realize then that I've forgotten what it's like to wrestle with God. What an absolutely human thing it is—and one that many of us have distracted ourselves from. Many of us not only don't wrestle with God but also don't even bother looking for him because we have so much we think we need to do. We are so busy doing that we miss out on some really important conversations with God. We cover our wrestles and wonderings about something bigger than ourselves with all the things that make *us* bigger and make God smaller. Maybe we lose faith because we no longer feel the need for it. Dare I say, these phones have made even the most devoted people gradually lose sight of their faith as they fix their sights on so many other things.

Allow me to let you into the wrestle that *being* led me toward. It was a wrestling match that felt like it came out of nowhere, but the reality is that doubt and confusion can exist in our hearts even before we raise the volume of God's voice in our lives. We're just too distracted to recognize it, much less wrestle with it. For me, the simple rhythms of life in the abbey created space for solitude, and that ended up triggering one of the most significant events in my faith journey. So in the next chapter, I want to invite you into that story, with the hope that it will help you when you find yourself face-to-face with your own wrestle.

CHAPTER 7
SOLITUDE

We were created with the wonderful capacity to wrestle with our conscience—the voice within that tells us what is right and wrong. And this wrestle normally happens when there is not a lot of outside noise invading our thoughts. This is something that is uniquely human. I mean, maybe my 130-pound Bernese Mountain Dog, Hawk, looks like he has a conscience after I get him in trouble for eating my breakfast off the table, but if I leave food on the table two minutes later and once again allow him to "wrestle with his conscience," he'll eat the food all over again. There is no contrition. There is no wrestling. There is just instinct.

We as humans, though, are built for this. We are created for wrestling and self-reflection—to enter our own thoughts and swim around in them. To let our minds wander. To sit for hours pondering everything from the details of our days to the deeper meaning of life. And if you are anything like me—at least like I was at the beginning of this experiment—there is little to no room left in your life to engage with the deeper parts of your thoughts and soul. For many of us, time for self-reflection is now available only in the few moments between putting our phones on the end tables next to our beds and closing our eyes—and that's just not enough. Perhaps this is starting to sound like I'm about to go all *ban the phones* here, but just go with me for a second.

I've done my best to avoid phone bashing. Again, I love a lot of what phones and screens have brought to us. But I also want to remind us of the things we've lost so we can reclaim them. And one of those things might initially feel scary. It may even feel like something we needed to get rid of because it can take us to places we may not want to go. I'm talking about solitude.

Solitude.

Just typing the word feels almost mysterious. Like this is something only super-spiritual people—like grown adults who live in monasteries or convents—chase after. Why in the world would the rest of us normal people want to chase after solitude? Well, maybe because God designed us with a need for solitude, which means it should be a regular occurrence in our lives. Solitude is what creates space for introspection. It's where we fine-tune our conscience—that ability not just to discern between right and wrong but also to think deeply about complicated moral issues. It's where we reconnect with ourselves—and maybe even wrestle with the parts of us that need to change and grow. It's also where we face our demons. The worries and wounds that we'd rather *not* have to think about.

Trying to avoid solitude is nothing new. We've always been drawn to distractions and diversions, because sitting alone with our thoughts can be *hard*. Way back in the 1600s Blaise Pascal said, "All the unhappiness of men arises from one single fact, that they cannot stay quietly in their own chamber."[1] But it's only in the last ten or so years that we've reached the point where it's possible to completely avoid and even eradicate solitude.

Seriously. Think about it.

The cross-pollination of smartphones and social media has ushered in something unprecedented in human history. We are connected to the entire world twenty-four hours a day, 365 days a year. By the standards of human history, *this is not normal*. It's not. Up until the last decade, most of us had at least some solitude built into our lives, whether we wanted it or not. It is now possible to completely eradicate solitude from your life. And with the eradication of solitude, we are left with a ridiculously diminished capacity for introspection and self-reflection.

Solitude is no longer required. The ability to never have solitude has arrived. *How crazy is that?* I'm hoping you can imagine my jaw hitting my keyboard because this realization is mind-blowing.

For most of human history, time alone with your own thoughts was not only a normal, multiple-times-a-day occurrence but inescapable. Traveling from point A to point B was never filled with anything other than our own thoughts. Lunch breaks were exactly that—a break. Nature walks were filled with nature, not consuming podcasts or audiobooks.

I believe that solitude is hardwired into the human experience. If you are a believer in something greater than yourself, you would say that God created us with solitude as a major pillar in our existence.

But we have wiped it out.

And you know what? It's not necessarily our relationship with our phones that is the problem. Dare I say that the root of the problem is our relationship with solitude? It's like when you hire a nutritionist, and after two days of eating great you slip back into old habits. And suddenly you begin avoiding this nutritionist at all costs. Even though you know this person is bringing you advice and accountability that's necessary and good for you, you would just rather be numb and lazy. Just like we know that a conversation with our nutritionist is going to call attention to our poor eating habits, we all know that time spent in solitude is going to call attention to things in our lives that we really don't want to confront.

Do you think that maybe we don't know what to do with the wrestling that solitude brings? A life without wrestling feels like a safer life, right? Well, maybe it's safer in some respects, but I can tell you that it's a dangerous threat when it comes to your ability to simply be.

I was seven days into my screen-free journey when my wrestle with solitude exploded. Listen, the first four days had been gutting—not because of the solitude per se but more because I was coming off the drug called my smartphone. I was legit having night sweats, heart palpitations, nightmares—all symptoms someone coming off a drug could have. I even felt sick. Like, achy. I assumed I was detoxing. It was awful.

But after a few days of grossness, on morning four it felt like an elephant stepped off my chest and I could breathe again. I was praying five times a day and enjoying my newly found serenity. The only uncomfortable thing that kept creeping up was the occasional inability to get out of my own head. I had the strangest feeling that I wanted to stop thinking about whatever it was I was thinking about—and that I needed my phone to do it.

One of the things having 24-7 access to the world through a screen gives us is the ability to avoid our own thoughts when they seem like too much. And I'm not talking about just bad thoughts—I'm talking about all the thoughts. Tasks, emails, to-dos, and all the rest. But I quickly realized that the only way for me to avoid my thoughts without my phone was to pick up the novel that I'd brought from home. When my mind began to race and I didn't have

TikTok to turn to, I read a story about an eighty-nine-year-old serial killer who was pretending to be a nursing home patient with dementia. *Yeah, great escape, Carlos.* I'm so good at choosing distractions.

But you know what happened on day five? I finished my novel. And that was the night my wrestle with solitude began. I was sitting on the sofa looking out over the silhouettes of trees that covered the abbey grounds, and I don't know why or how, but every possible scary and worry-filled thought I could have entered my mind at the same time. All of my worries and fears about my family came flooding in.

Does Losiah know how much I love him and that I would do anything for him?

Is Sohaila really healed from her lung issues, or is there something secretly waiting in the corner of her body ready to strike and send our family back into panic?

Does Seanna trust me even though I have broken my word to her too many times to count?

Does Heather really forgive me for all of the pain I've caused her?

Is this pain in my left arm a heart attack or did I just pull something?

And then the scope of the worries got even bigger. I started to wonder about God and his ability to solve the issues in my life, since he didn't seem to be doing much to solve bigger issues around the globe. I mean, mass shootings? Human trafficking? Regional wars all over the planet? American politics? The world seems more broken and divided than ever before, and it sometimes feels like it's hanging by a thread.

These are all thoughts we like to avoid, right? I mean, who in their right mind *wants* to dwell on these things? The problem for me on day five was that I couldn't stop thinking about them, and I had nothing that could help me stop. Until it hit me.

"My journal!" I yelled. I found it on the kitchen table and started scribbling.

God, I don't know what to do with all of this in my head. Like, all of these thoughts are starting to make me doubt. *Doubt you.* I'm at a freaking monastery hanging around with monks all day, and I can't get past the fact that I'm starting to doubt not only that you hear my prayers but that you will ever have time to.

There is a difficulty I'm facing. All of this pain and suffering—most of it undeserved by my family, myself, and the world at large—is presenting a huge conundrum for me. Are you good? Are you God? How do I come to the conclusion that the answer to both of these questions is yes, especially in the face of such a terrifying history of humanity? My question is shifting from, "How can a loving God permit so much evil in the world?" to "Does all the evil in the world even allow for the possibility that a loving God exists?

You see, friend, this is what I am talking about. Who wants this sort of stuff to be occupying our thoughts when we can simply silence them by consuming the thoughts of others online? Well, can I answer my own question? Um, actually, I can because I'm writing the book.

The answer to our inability to enjoy and exist in solitude isn't to look at God less, but maybe it's admitting our understanding of him may be less. Less than we had originally thought.

I shut off the lights, climbed into bed, pulled the sheets over my head, and let out a yell I can only assume made any monks who might have heard it conclude I was being murdered—or that I was experiencing exactly what they thought I was experiencing. I leaned to the latter. Maybe they'd all taken bets about when exactly my meltdown would occur. I imagined their conversation at the sound of my scream went something along the lines of, "Ah, there it is! Brother John Baptist, you had his meltdown occurring on day three. Father Francis, you picked day seven. Brother Dominic, you had him not melting down at all. But Father Joseph, you nailed it— day five! You win the bet this week."

The next morning at breakfast, I broke the silence protocol and walked straight up to Father Francis. "I can't wait until Saturday. Can I please talk to you today?"

"What's the problem, Carlos?" he replied.

"I'm starting to be scared that my belief in God is waning. Like, I believe in God. But all this suffering?" I said with my voice trembling and looking past him to avoid seeing the disappointment in his eyes. There was none. In fact, his expression brightened up a bit, and I thought I saw his eyes smile without his mouth even moving.

"Ah, I see," he said kindly. "Come to my office today at 4:00 p.m. I can make time. But before you come, I want you to go on a hike or something. Go on a walk. Maybe to the cemetery and watch the storm roll in this morning. Just make sure to hike back down before it hits."

He was right. Being cooped up in a library or in my cabin while my mind was spinning and my understanding of God was swaying probably wasn't the best idea. When I walked out of his office, this simple question hit me: *Is it God that I am having a hard time with, or is it the smallness of God that is getting in my way?*

Woah.

I skipped breakfast and started hiking toward the cemetery.

My daily hikes were spent mostly looking for animals—coyotes, quail, roadrunners. (Yes, they are real. Why did it take me until my late forties to realize that?) But today I wasn't looking for animals. I was looking for God.

Solitude had brought me to some really intrusive thoughts. But on my hike I began to wonder if maybe they weren't intrusive after all. Maybe they were thoughts and questions that had always been there, but I had silenced them by picking up my phone every time they tried to get my attention.

As I got closer to the top of the hill, I could clearly see the thunderheads forming in the distance. The sky was marvelous. The wind was beginning to pick up, and I could feel a few small drops of rain hitting my face. I quickened my pace.

I want you to think about something for a minute. What might you have lost because of the absence of solitude in your life? Is it thinking of something bigger than yourself? Is it being able to dream of moments that you can create with your kids? Is it being able to hear the voice of God in your life? It could be many things, but I want you to think about this on purpose. *What has been lost in your life because of your inability to have solitude?*

The fact that we are constantly connected has also shifted and changed the way that we perceive and value solitude. Maybe you are having a hard time even imagining it as a good thing. That's okay! But I hope you are sensing that it's something that's not only important but actually necessary.

Get this. Studies have shown that being constantly connected has led to increased loneliness in society.[2] That we can constantly compare our lives with others' idealized lives can fuel feelings of inadequacy and self-doubt. FOMO is *real*. You know who didn't have FOMO? *Anyone who doesn't have a phone.* Recovering our ability to have regular solitude is so important for our mental health and overall well-being.

And the good news is, we don't have to go too far back to get practical insights and lessons on how to do this solitude thing well.

Here are a few ways you can reclaim solitude today.

1. **WAKE UP BEFORE THE SUN**. Yes, there are always going to be emails and notifications waiting for you, but when you arise before the rest of your collective community, you have a chance to start the day knowing that nobody is waiting for a response, and you have an opportunity to just *be*.

2. **COMMUTE IN SILENCE**. I know it's crazy to imagine this one. Sometimes our car rides or train rides are the only minutes during the day that we have to ourselves. So we often think this would be the best time to consume and enjoy the things that we want to enjoy. And for many of us, yes, it's a great time to self-improve.

    I'm not saying get rid of your self-improvement time altogether, but start with two out of five daily commutes when you just let your mind wander. Let solitude take over and see what happens. Many times the best type of self-improvement will happen only when you actually spend time with your *self*.

3. **EXPERIMENT ON YOURSELF**. Listen, I know I lived at a monastery for two weeks and an Amish farm for two weeks, but you don't have to do that. What if you had regular, twenty-four-hour digital detoxes that you could step into and experience just a glimmer of solitude? This would remind yourself that solitude isn't something to be scared of but rather it's something that you need.

4. **EXPERIMENT WITH TECH-FREE HOBBIES**. One of the reasons I love to fly-fish is that it is practically impossible to fly-fish and hold a phone. It forces me to solitude in ways that I can't have when I'm connected. What sort of activity can you do that takes both of your hands and also places you in a space where a screen isn't involved? I mean, quite literally this could be as simple as decorating your yard for Christmas or learning to work on your car. Both of these are

activities that push me into solitude because I'm using both my hands and am away from screens. Some of my best ideas have come either on my roof or under my car!

You don't have to move to a monastery. I did that for you. Now just do solitude on purpose. Every day. You were made for this . . .

Reclaiming some sort of solitude in your life may seem almost impossible. But let me tell you something. I'm currently writing this book almost a year after I did this experiment, and not only is solitude available to you, it's going to produce more living your life instead of your life living you.

———

When I made it to the top of the hill, I walked over to this gigantic monument that the monks call the Eye of the Needle. Imagine a thirty-foot-high and ten-foot-wide stone rectangle, and chiseled out of the center is an oval large enough for a human to stand in. The bottom of the oval is about ten feet off the ground. After a couple of late-forties-man attempts to climb up and sit in the oval, I finally made it. I sat there in the Eye of the Needle and just stared at the sky. *Why did Father Francis tell me to come up here?*

I spoke out loud the question that had popped in my head as I left his office: "Is it God that I am having a hard time with, or is it the smallness of God that is getting in my way?"

I pulled out my journal and started reading what I'd written the night before, all of which revolved around the heartache and evil in the world and how an all-powerful God could allow such suffering. But when I looked up at the storm rolling in, I felt a sense of awe and wonder. I could feel the grandness of God in the thunderheads, in the wind that was pressing against my face. If he is felt and exists in this storm, in the grand and marvelous things, then surely he must exist in the broken and small things as well, right? Maybe he is in the suffering. Or more likely he is simply *with* the suffering. Something about this storm began to fill my lungs with breath again. It was almost impossible to see the grandness of what was in front of me and deny that God exists.

"Look up," I said. I don't know where it came from, but I said it aloud again. "Look up."

I am usually so consumed by the thing in my hands that I seldom look up to see what God is doing all around me. How much of my view of God is based on what I see on the seven inches of LCD that I hold in my hands every day? How much of my theology is simply read or watched online and not experienced personally?

I did some mental calculations and realized I had not existed in a space of solitude for fifteen years. That was when I got my first BlackBerry that could connect to the World Wide Web at any moment of the day. And that was when solitude slowly began to get choked out of my life.

"You have spent the last fifteen years *holding* the world in your hand and have stopped *beholding* me in the world."

Wait, what?!

As clear as I have ever thought I heard a voice, while knowing full well I didn't *hear* a voice, I heard those words. I believe it was God.

Maybe it wasn't that I had stopped believing in God. Maybe it was that there wasn't enough room in my life to actually *see* all that I wanted to *believe*.

And it took solitude for me to get here.

"Behold," I said. "So I gotta start to *behold*."

The raindrops that had started falling a few minutes earlier began to come down more consistently. No more spattering. Now it was actually beginning to rain. I dropped my backpack to the ground ten feet below and prepared to late-forties-man maneuver myself to the ground, a move that would have been more of a leap fifteen years ago. I had decided to spend the day hiking even farther up into the hills behind the cemetery before my meeting with Father Francis.

I needed to practice *beholding*.

CHAPTER 8

BEHOLDING

I had spent a week praying five times a day with monks, and I was having some God-size doubts invade my head. I was also having another crisis at the exact same time—one of my own doing. Have you ever found yourself in a crisis brought on by your own stupidity? Your own inability to make grown-up decisions?

I was on top of this mountain, it was now pouring rain, and as I slid down the wet monument, one of my flip-flops broke. Specifically, the little part that goes between your big toe and the next toe.[i]

So the toe thong part of my flip-flop came out of the little hole it lives in. And I don't know if you know this or not, but without it being attached, *there is no flip-flop*. Like, there is no way for it to flip or flop. It may as well be a tiny doormat because it doesn't move with your body.

Here I was, at the top of this mountain, hundreds of headstones all around me, and only one flip-flop. The entire path back

---

i. Which *should* be called the big toe, right? Because that next toe is actually taller than the thumb toe. At least mine is. Is that not normal? Is your second toe not taller than your thumb toe?

down the desert road was nothing but rocks. And you should know that all through elementary school, I was called Carlos Tenderfoot Whittaker because I could barely walk on grass without wincing in pain. It usually took me twenty minutes to hike from the cemetery back down to the abbey, but today it took me an hour. I. Wish. You. Could. Have. Seen. Me. I was not only wincing with every single step but I was also making sounds. I'm so freaking dramatic. It was like having a man-cold but in my foot.

⸺

Four o'clock came sooner rather than later, and I nervously made my way to Father Francis's office. I had not yet entered a monk's office. *Do monks even have offices? Maybe he has one because he used to be the abbot.* It was above the used bookstore. The one I'd broken into, remember?

When I cracked the door, I was greeted with a giant hug and a welcoming, "Hello, young man!" There's nothing that makes a forty-eight-year-old man feel younger than being called a young man. Do yourself a favor and start hanging out with people older than you.

The office walls were lined with books. His desk was stacked with books. I sat in a leather chair across the desk from Father Francis and looked him in the eyes from the valley of books that he had carved out to see his guests.

"So how was your walk?" Father Francis asked.

"I broke my flip-flop at the cemetery, but besides that everything was amazing," I joked.

He smiled and then just stared at me. I was here to listen to him, to receive the life-changing words that would flow from his mouth to my heart and fix my broken faith. But he continued staring. Not saying anything. *Um, okay. This is getting weird. I guess I need to say a bit more.*

"So, Father, this whole faith thing. The reason I came up to talk to you . . . well, I suddenly had the thought that maybe my view of God was too small. And that was really compelling. It got me thinking. And I was thinking a *lot* at the top of the hill. The word that kept coming to me was *behold*. Like, I almost audibly heard that I need to *behold*. But then I wonder, *Was that God or was that just me thinking to myself?*

I felt as if the books surrounding me were beginning to close in on me. With every passing word the room grew smaller and my words formed faster.

"I mean, I have traveled the world teaching people to hear the voice of God, and then I show up here at this monastery and I suddenly start feeling seeds of doubt creep in. Like, the gospel is a *really crazy story*, right? It's crazy when you think about it. And all the pain and suffering in the world. Look at all the crises. How could a good God let all of that happen? I'm just having a hard time right now. I mean—"

"Carlos," interrupted Father Francis. His eyes were smiling. Almost like he knew I was exactly where I needed to be. "You said you heard the word *behold* while you were up on the mountain?" I noticed that he kept calling it a mountain and I kept calling it a hill.

"Have you ever heard the quote, 'The glory of God is man fully alive'?"

"Yes, yes I have," I replied.

"Well, there is a second part to that quote by Saint Irenaeus. It keeps going. It says, 'And the life of the human consists in beholding God.'"[1]

I had never heard that part of the quote before. I'd always heard the first part, that the glory of God is revealed in a human being fully alive. But never the second part—that our life should consist of beholding God. *Wow*.

"I don't think we need hours of conversation inside these four walls for you to find God again," Father Francis said. "Because I don't think you have actually ever lost him."

When he referred to the four walls, he had gestured to the walls of his office. These were walls I could not even see because they were covered with hundreds and hundreds of books—all of which I assumed Father Francis had read. I mean, he was certainly old enough to have read them all. This man had been a monk for over fifty years. He had walked at God speed, prayed all day every day, and existed in a life of obedience and reverence for longer than I had been alive. He didn't look the least bit fazed by my crisis.

Now I was the one silently staring as Father Francis continued to talk.

He talked about the greatness of God. He talked about not being scared to look at the things we don't understand about God just because they make us doubt. I noticed that when he was talking, God seemed so *big*. Not small. And I wanted that perspective so bad. As Father Francis continued, his words were as easy as Sunday morning. With every passing moment I felt a bit more belief begin to form in my chest.

Then, after just fifteen minutes of conversation, Father Francis abruptly stood up and said, "Thanks for stopping by, Carlos. I'll see you at dinner."

Behold—that word is an announcement of something grand. And although the pain and sorrow I kept thinking about were real, thanks to Father Francis's words, I began to sense that if I could just zoom out a little and gain some perspective, I'd also see the reality of the grandness of God.

I had a new mission. For an entire day I was going to find

something that I had a hard time believing about his grandness, and I was gonna test it.

When I left Father Francis's office, I walked straight downstairs to the used bookstore. I had seen a book there a few days ago, and it immediately came to mind when I felt challenged to test something I was having a hard time believing about the grandness of God. I remembered the cover had a photo of the solar system on it. It was called *The First Three Minutes: A Modern View of the Origin of the Universe*. It was all about the Big Bang—the theory that the universe was created by an explosion. It was a topic I had always avoided because I was scared that if I looked into it too deeply, it would erase my belief in God.

To be honest, I didn't just walk to the bookstore; I almost marched with fists clenched like an angry toddler being told to go to his room. I marched quickly, even though I feared the end of my faith might be only a few minutes away. I was ready to read this book explaining away God.

Part of the beauty of the abbey's used bookstore is that it's all donated books, most of which are Catholic in nature. But I had seen this one at the top of a box, which I assumed meant the monks had yet to sort it and decide if it would make it onto the shelves. I also assumed that this book wasn't going to make the cut—I was pretty sure it was full of stuff that ran counter to what Catholic monks believed.[ii] Suffice to say that in that moment, I was ready for an epic battle between faith and science. And for a long time leading up to that moment, I'd felt genuinely concerned that science might land some truly faith-shaking punches. I'd been avoiding these doubts for too long.

---

ii. Little did I know that the Big Bang theory was originally proposed by a Roman Catholic priest in the 1920s, or that Pope Pius XII had declared the Big Bang theory to be compatible with the Christian doctrine of creation! This isn't the right setting to dig into all of that, though.

I grabbed the book and headed back to my hot cabin.

Taking a deep breath, I opened the book and began reading what Steven Weinberg, a Nobel Prize–winning physicist, had to say about what happened at the beginning of the universe and how we know about it.

Before I tell you what I read in the first few pages of a book that I assumed could be the beginning of the end of everything I had ever believed, I want to ask you a question: How much is the device that you keep in your pocket—or the one you may even be using to read or listen to this book right now—making God smaller than you want him to be? You may not have ever thought about it like this, but stay with me.

Perhaps you follow social media accounts that give you tidbits of inspiration here and there—maybe they post Bible verses and cool thirty-second sermon clips with background hype music that give you a little inspiration for the moment. But really, truly, are your screens adding to the greatness of God in your life? Or are they reducing God to a sound bite?

During my screen-free experiment, I found that even the uplifting, spiritually oriented content that I tended to consume via screens often minimized God rather than making him bigger. Not always, but far too often. The truth we all know is that no matter how much work someone puts into an Instagram post and no matter what music is embedded behind the reel (even if it is a favorite song that draws us nearer to God whenever we listen to it), no social media post comes anywhere close to touching the reality of the greatness of God. I will even go out on a limb and say that the content we typically consume on our phones should be way down the list when it comes to how we experience God. It's definitely behind the great outdoors, the Bible itself, and being in community with people who build your faith. Social media and YouTube videos can be a great peripheral. But we cannot rely on the virtual world offered by screens if we're really seeking to behold the greatness of God.

⎯⎯

Spoiler alert: I'm about to give away where I landed after reading the Big Bang book, but you're going to want to keep reading to see how an astrophysicist convinced me all over again to believe in God. However, first I want to let you know about three ways I learned to behold God during the two months I spent away from my phone.

1. **SIT AND CONTEMPLATE THE GRANDNESS AND MAJESTY OF GOD'S CREATION**. Make sure that you find a way every single day (it's possible!) to *behold* the grandness and majesty of the world around you. Cathedrals and man-made spiritual buildings can invoke some beholding from us, but *nothing* like the grandness of God's creation. And I'm not just talking about hiking the Grand Canyon. Yes, you can behold that. But have you ever sat and stared at a honeybee on a flower? That right there is just as grand and miraculous a creation. I promise, even if you live in a concrete jungle, you can behold him. Go outside—right now—and behold.

2. **READ BEHOLD STORIES IN THE WORD OF GOD**. I know you may or may not believe in the Bible as I do, and that is fine. I've had people who don't share my faith tell me that they still enjoy reading the scriptures I sometimes talk about because they find peace or guidance in them. So however you view the Bible, I encourage you to read a few of its stories of individuals who experienced these *behold* moments of awe and wonder. I mean, Mary, the mother of Jesus, had an angel show up and literally say, "And *behold*, you will

conceive in your womb and bring forth a Son, and shall call His name Jesus" (Luke 1:31 NKJV). Talk about a behold moment! In the Old Testament there's Moses. He had *lots* of behold moments, perhaps none of which was as crazy as seeing the angel of the Lord in a burning bush that didn't burn up.

Here are a few passages to get you started. You'll notice that when you see the word *behold* in the Bible, it's normally announcing something grand, as Father Francis put it.

Therefore the Lord Himself will give you a sign. *Behold*, the virgin shall conceive and bear a Son, and shall call His name Immanuel.

ISAIAH 7:14 NKJV

Behold, I am doing a new thing;
now it springs forth, do you not perceive it?
I will make a way in the wilderness and
rivers in the desert.

ISAIAH 43:19 ESV

Then the angel said to them, "Do not be afraid, for *behold*, I bring you good tidings of great joy which will be to all people."

LUKE 2:10 NKJV

"*Behold!* The Lamb of God who takes away the sin of the world!"

JOHN 1:29 NKJV

The number of times I've seen something in Scripture that reminds me God is greater than I could ever imagine are too many to count. Sometimes we just need to be reminded of how awe-inspiring God really is.

3. **CHASE AFTER THINGS THAT SCARE YOU ABOUT GOD.** The things you tend to avoid researching because maybe it will lead you to a crisis of faith. I can promise you this: God isn't scared of our faith crises. He's not scared of our deconstruction. Sometimes we have to ask the hard questions to dismantle ideas we've had about God that have made him too small. So that undoing is necessary. I've found that God has become *much* bigger after I've asked the hard questions. *Go for it!* He's not worried. He can handle them.

There was a lot of stuff *way* over my head and above my non-astrophysicist pay grade in the Big Bang book. And to be honest, I made it only about forty pages before I closed it. Not because it wasn't fascinating or well written but because I had learned all I needed to learn about the Big Bang. Now, I need to say something before I give you my thoughts about what I read. If you believe in the Big Bang, then I'm in no way saying you shouldn't. I'm simply saying what I got out of this book, which was written to explain a really complicated theory about the origins of the universe.

According to people a lot smarter than me, something happened between 13 and 16 billion years ago, which is some crazy math. There was this nursery of stars—a stellar nursery. And this stellar nursery was over 80 quintillion miles away. One of the stars in this nursery was what they called a neutron star. And this star weighed a million tons per teaspoon. A black hole nearby sucked this neutron star into it and exploded the neutron star with such force that within a few milliseconds after the explosion, it created the universe we now live in. That explosion was so huge that even physicists today still can't really explain how huge it was. Kind of unexplainable, even to them.

Kind of unexplainable.

While reading all the research behind the Big Bang, I was suddenly hit with a realization I wasn't expecting. I put the book down and looked out into the desert sky. And in my first moment of beholding, I thought, *So the idea that the universe was created by a large explosion is actually, for me at least, more unbelievable than Jesus dying and coming back to life.* I thought the Big Bang book might seal my unbelief, but instead I now felt even more certain that there was something far greater than a neutron star out there—that there was more to the design of the universe than an accidental black-hole explosion. The order of the stars. The order of the planets. The order of the animals. The order of our bodies. The order of all of it. It's all so miraculous.

There is so much order in creation that I found it impossible to believe the universe came from disorder. I kept looking at the sky outside. At the trees swaying over the building. The hawk circling overhead. Instead of losing my faith, reading the book convinced me that there was an overwhelming case that the universe was created by someone much greater than I am. And it was by asking the hard question, by beholding, that I found my way back to him.

Did beholding answer all my questions about suffering? No. But did it cement the idea that there is something much greater than me running this whole universe thing? Absolutely.

After dinner and evening prayers, I stopped by the cabin to grab one of the plastic chairs from my front porch and then continued hiking the trail back up to the top of the ridge. I wanted to watch the sun set and the stars appear.

I saw my first star at around 9:00 p.m. Shortly after, I saw a shooting star that flew clear across the sky. Like, from one side to the other. All the way. And then another. And another. Over thirty minutes I counted thirty-eight stars flying around in the heavens above.

Behold, I sit in the midst of the most majestic cathedral I've ever been in.

God was showing off for me. And I'd never been more convinced of something in my entire life.

Behold.

CHAPTER 9

CONTROL

Just as I was beginning to find my pace with monastic life, my time at the abbey was drawing to a close. Those last few nights I sat on my front porch, watching the sunset and mourning the end of my visit. I encountered so much that changed me—so many moments that made me think, *Man, I wish I could be a monk. If only I could be a monk and still be married to Heather.* So I guess I wasn't going to become a monk. But the monks' practices had centered me in ways I'd never experienced before. I guess I hadn't known how much my world was spinning until I got to the abbey and left the phone behind. It's as if I hadn't known I wasn't breathing until I got here—and now that I was, I didn't want to lose the breath in my lungs.

Perhaps the biggest change was that I was trusting God more than I ever had before. I hadn't realized how much trust in God I'd lost because of the ways I relied on the screen in my pocket instead. And I'm not talking about big trust things. I'm talking about the daily things a lot of us once trusted God with. For example, when we're facing uncertainty about a major life decision or notice a worrisome medical symptom, we can quickly go to Google, hoping to calm our fears or find answers—but we forget all about the fact that we can go to God in prayer. We've grown accustomed to trusting the sound bite from the podcast we just listened to, but we should be going straight to God to ask him for wisdom.

Or how about the way smartphones allow us to track our kids' every move? I understand that supervising kids is a challenge, and modern technology offers all kinds of solutions. But are we allowing these new technologies to give us the illusion of control? And is that illusion undermining our ability to trust God?

Listen, before I get going here, let me address the objection you might be about to DM me: "The world is more dangerous than it used to be, Carlos. We need to take precautions." I get it, and you're right. Our smartphones definitely give us peace of mind in ways my parents' generation would probably have loved, right? Well, I can assume. Or I could just ask. So I asked my mom.

Specifically, I asked her about Life360, the family tracking app that not only allows you to see where all your family members are but also sends parents alerts about their kid's driving habits or when it detects a car crash. She knows what Life360 is because she's on mine now. As she and my dad get older, I want to make sure I can get to them if something happens.

"Mom, do you wish you had something like Life360 when I was growing up?" I asked.

"I don't know," she said. "I have a tendency to worry, and I feel like maybe an app like that would have made me worry even more. When you and your friends went somewhere, your dad and I used to just have to trust that things would be okay. Once in a while they weren't, and we eventually found out."

Her response initially surprised me, but I think she's right. In fact, I think gaining the smartphone has caused us not only to lose trust in something greater than ourselves but also makes us feel like we are in control of our lives. And both things—losing trust and believing we're in control—are problematic.

Our phones offer so many benefits, but deluding us into thinking we are in control of our lives is not one of them. What gives us that delusion? Well, think about it. We can manage our tasks. We can plan and schedule our family calendars with wicked precision. We can connect with anyone we want, anywhere we want, anytime we want. We can control our lights, our heating, and even our appliances. We can track how fast or slow our kids are driving. We can quickly access lots of information, which deludes us into thinking we're masters of things that have taken the actual masters decades to master. All of this creates the sense that we are like Mickey Mouse in *Fantasia*, waving our magic wand (phone) in every direction and the world around us just jumping to obey.

But may I tell you something, amigos and amigas?

Control is a façade. It is, really. You are no more in control of your life today than your great-great-grandparents were in control of their lives one hundred years ago. I'm here to be the bubble buster. As hard as it may be to do this, I need you to stick out your control bubble and let me pop it. Because it's empty. It is. You aren't in control. And here's the reason it's so important to pop that bubble: it's only when you finally surrender your control bubble to something or someone much greater than yourself that you get a trust bubble—one that can actually be filled up with something true and substantial.

While surrendering control might sound scary, it's also incredibly freeing. Having to control everything is exhausting. When you finally realize you aren't in control and you choose to trust something or someone greater than yourself, there is instant relief. Ah! The freedom you find is life-giving.

———

"You used to get on your bike and ride to your friend Brian's house," my mom said. "And I used to tell you to come home by the time the streetlights turned on. Most days you made it home on time. The few times you didn't, I got in my car, worried, but I always found you. I guess if I'd had Life360 back then, I wouldn't have had to get in my car. But I also would have been looking at that app a lot more, checking where you were instead of focusing on dinner. Maybe I wouldn't have worried as much, but dinners would also have been a lot worse." My mom was on a roll.

"I think I trusted God a lot more then than I do now," she said. "Now, it feels like we can trust Google."

Hello, Carmen Whittaker! Could you please pick up the microphone you just dropped?!

And ain't what she said the truth? Think about it. We go straight to Google with every single ailment we have, only to find out that, according to WebMD, we have just three days to live before this incredibly rare disease takes us out. Why is Google the first place we go? Because that's what we trust.

We trust Google more than God. Google > God.

But for Mom, it's God > Google.

(Can someone put "God > Google" on a bumper sticker, stat?)

Our phones have us fooled!

———

Let's talk about hesitation for a minute. Without trust in God and his promises, we end up hesitating so much more, right? We hesitate and wait when we should be trusting and moving. Sometimes I wonder how many of Jesus' disciples would have dropped their nets and followed him if they'd been able to check him out on Instagram before he showed up. Would they have even gone out to hear him speak if they'd watched all his YouTube sermons and read the negative comments left by people who critique sermons full-time?

Hesitation is a consequence of believing we are in control. When it comes to God, since we have so many answers at our fingertips in Google, we crave more tangible assurance of God and his ways. And when the proof isn't evident and doesn't show up right away, what do we do? We start grasping at control to give us a false sense of safety. And our phones provide the means of that control. But while we're waiting for all the answers we need to fall into place or endlessly researching the bottomless pit of information and opinions that is the internet, we end up frozen. Not moving. Not risking. Waiting for blessed assurance before we take one step toward where we were supposed to be going in faith a long time ago.

It's like the fact that *everything* is readily available on Amazon (convenient, right?) but there's also a mind-boggling number of options and plenty of contradictory reviews (not so convenient). What used to be a quick trip to a nearby store to choose between just a couple of available options can turn into days of obsessively researching and second-guessing before finally clicking the Buy button. That's just a small example, but it illustrates the point I'm making. Immediate access to endless options (and endless, contradictory reviews about those options) might seem like control at first. But it's not actually all that empowering to sit there, hesitating to take the leap before reading one more review or checking out one more product from another manufacturer!

If you've been waiting for "the right time" to trust God and do the next thing, my question to you is, How much time are you spending in his Word versus on your phone? Listen, I am the king of spending time with my phone, so I ask the question with no judgment. However, I do ask it with plenty of experience, and here's why: when we aren't connected to the world 24-7, we actually *have* to exist in a place of trust.

I learned this life lesson on day ten of my experience at the monastery, when I got a message to call home as soon as possible. Something was happening in my family that needed my input. It needed my prayers. It needed my advice. It needed me.

"Okay, I'll come home," I said to my daughter. "I can get a ride to the airport and get home by tomorrow morning."

"Dad, don't be silly," she said. "You don't need to come home. I just needed your advice. I'll be okay."

But I wanted to go home. Why? Because it gave me the illusion that, somehow, I would be more in control of the situation if I was at home than if I was at the monastery. But the truth is, that's a big *fat* lie. I would be no more in control of the situation while being at home than I was on the phone. The real problem was with me. I knew I was not going to have 24-7 access to my daughter while I was at the abbey. I was going to have to *trust* God to do the thing I said I had always trusted him to do but desperately wanted to do myself. I was stuck. I *had* to trust. I had no phone. I had no laptop. I had no Apple Watch. I had no way of constantly checking in.

I. Was. Not. In. Control.

And that is the reality in your life as well. The phone in your pocket does not give you the control you think it gives you. It's a trick.

Hanging up the phone with my daughter, handing her over to God, and trusting that he could take care of her way better than I ever could was difficult. But it would have been next to impossible to trust God that way if I'd been able to contact her whenever I wanted to.

How's all this talk about trust and control hitting? A little different, right? Maybe it feels too close to home—like I'm attacking *you* as opposed to your habits. If so, I get it. Popping my control bubble felt like that for me too. But I promise you, it's worth it. The end result is more freedom and less fear. So let's get after it.

In what ways have you chosen to take control of your life rather than to trust God with it? Have you stopped asking God what the next steps of your business should be and instead turned to business podcasts to give you direction? Have you allowed WebMD to be the tool that you use to calm your fears instead of going to God with all of your worries? I want you to name what trusting God in that situation means for you. For example, is your trust dependent on God coming through for you in every single thing you ask him to do? Because I know what that feels like. There was a season in my life when I was so angry that God didn't come through for me that I wrote him off. But let's think about that for a second. When we relinquish control, why might God still choose not to come through in the specific ways that we ask or hope?

Let's flip to the gospel. When it seems like God doesn't intervene in our affairs, we can think about what he did with his own Son. He let his Son be mercilessly murdered on a cross without any intervention because his plan for Jesus was greater than anyone at the time could understand. Even Jesus, who knew about this big plan, had a moment of wrestling with grief and fear as that trial loomed closer (Matthew 26:36–46).

In other words, just because you trust God does not automatically mean he is going to pull off what you want him to pull off.

Most of the time, we choose trust over control only when we have run out of options and are desperate for something, for anything.

When Google has not pulled off its heroics, when WebMD is wrong, when the podcast life hacks don't work, when the funny cat videos on TikTok no longer makes us laugh, when Life360 shows an alert that there has been an accident—this is when trust has to take over. Because that's when we finally remember that we and our little screens are not really in control.

So what are you going to do when that happens? How are you going to relinquish the control that is ultimately getting in the way of trust? A few options:

1. **TURN OFF THE TRACKING APPS**. I know, I know. It's a crazy thought. But maybe we weren't meant to always know exactly where our loved ones are. We think it will bring us peace, but I can tell you that I have also seen it create suspicion and misunderstanding. We still use Life360 for our teen drivers. But the better they get at driving, the less I look at it. And once I realized I wasn't looking at it all the time, I knew it was time to shut it off. There are still ways we can use technology to keep our kids safe; I just don't know if forever tracking their every move is one of them. I know I may get some pushback on this, but just as trusting in technology can hinder trust with God, it can also hinder trust with our kids. *Oof.*

2. **LET GOD HAVE YOUR DOUBT**. Truly. I'm not saying we have to do an about-face in one moment and suddenly become the spitting image of trust. It's okay to take things one step at a time. Start by identifying something you're trying to keep complete control of. For example, what if you actually went to Scripture instead of Google to counteract your worries about money? There can be real value in researching and implementing a financial plan, but why not start by going to the places in the Bible where God tells us that he is going

to provide for us no matter what? If you don't start with a foundation of trust in God, you may find yourself in a worry spiral. Doing the math over and over and obsessing about how things will turn out isn't control—it's a trap. And only trust can help you overcome that trap.

What if you actually asked God in a prayer to take back control of your life? What if you told him that you are tired of trying to be the one in control all the time? Whatever it is, give it to him and let him know any fears or concerns you have about giving it to him. Sometimes I live as if I suspect he just can't handle all the doubts and fears that I'm wrestling with. And the funny thing is, I leave that suspicion unsaid, as if he doesn't already know. If you're worrying that God can't handle your doubts, you need to hear this: *he can.* Give him your objections, doubts, and fears. Tell him that you don't believe. And then ask him to help you believe.

3. **DEVOTE ONE-TENTH OF THE TIME YOU SPEND ON A SCREEN TO READING THE BIBLE**. Seriously. If you spend five hours (three hundred minutes) a day on your phone, spend thirty minutes a day in the Scriptures. Because I'm good at math, as you know, here's the equation. Just plug in your numbers.

_____ x 60 = _____
(hours you spend on your phone)   (minutes you spend on your phone)

_____ x 0.10 = _____
(minutes you spend on your phone)   (minutes to spend reading the Bible)

I mean it; spend one-tenth of the time you are on your phone each day reading the sacred text. And if that feels like too much, make it one-fifteenth (just put 0.067 in the second equation instead of 0.10). Let's just start there. If you've got a smartphone, there's probably a calculator on it, so I'll let you do the math for yourself, because 0.067 is an odd number and I'm gonna mess that up big-time.

Remember, phones aren't bad. I love that I can know if my mom has been in a wreck before the paramedics know. This is a good thing. But what I don't want us to do is continue to think we are somehow in control of this life. We are tiny specks on a planet that rotates at a speed of about one thousand miles per hour while simultaneously orbiting around the sun at a speed of about sixty-seven thousand miles per hour. How could we think we are somehow in control of our lives?

We aren't.

And I want you to know that it's okay.

Because God *is* in control, and he can be trusted.

Turning off Find My iPhone in three, two, one. . . .

Okay, maybe not, because then how could I actually find my iPhone?

CHAPTER 10
PRESENCE

By day ten I was a professional pretend monk. I had it down. I was in the chapel before the first monk for all hours of prayer. I was helping new guests find their way around the monastery. I had inside-joked with the nun who was also the abbey accountant. I had named all of the ducks in the pond. I was basically a monk, except for the fact I was going to leave in a few days and be married and stuff. But besides those two important details—the leaving and the being married thing—I felt like a monk.

And may I tell you one of the most incredible realizations I had? It hit me on the morning of the tenth day when I was talking with another monk, named Brother Thomas. Halfway through our conversation, in the middle of me telling him a story about one of my kids, his eyes suddenly got a little wider and I saw him stop listening to me. Like, I saw it happen in his eyes. And as his eyes gave away the fact that his ears had shut off, I saw his left hand reach into the pocket of his robe. He then slipped out his cell phone and looked down at it.

"I'm so sorry, Carlos," he said. "I was making sure that wasn't my mother. She isn't feeling the best, and I hadn't heard from her all morning."

I was not bothered at all. "No worries, man. I get it. I wish I could check on my mom right now too!" I joked. And we kept going. And then about three minutes later, I heard his phone ding. Brother Thomas must have taken it off silent, but he didn't look at it this time. And I could see in his eyes that he didn't leave our conversation. "That's an email," he said. "Keep going."

But this time I was a little more baffled. Not bothered, may I remind you. But baffled. I was baffled that here I stood, talking to a monk, in the middle of this monastery, in the middle of the desert, and in the middle of me sharing my heart with him, we were interrupted by someone or something that was nowhere near us. It could have been a human one thousand miles away or it could have been an ad for a new truck. I don't know what it was. But what I did know is that this monk, this man of God who lives here full-time and devotes his life to prayer and service to the community, was being alerted by people nowhere near us and had to work overtime to keep his attention where it belonged. *The monks have a phone problem too!*

And that was when it hit me. I had just spent ten days experiencing complete and total presence with whomever was in front of me. God included. I had never, not once, been interrupted by someone who was nowhere near me while being in front of somebody who was very near me. I was actually shook. I couldn't recall the last time that had happened—the last time I went an entire day without a notification.

I'd had hundreds of conversations at the abbey by this point. With monks and non-monks. With nuns and housekeeping staff. With therapists and farmers. All sorts of people visited the halls of this abbey. And not once, not a single time, had I looked away from them while talking to them. They may have looked away from me a few times, but I don't think I noticed until my conversation with Brother Thomas. *A monk got pulled from the present moment and into an alternate universe.* Okay, so not really an alternate universe, but kind of. Like, he went into his head and away from me.

Ten days. This had to be some sort of Guinness World Record, right?

—————

Presence. Just like noticing, wondering, and solitude, presence is something that has all but evaporated from the human experience. We don't know how to be present anymore. I witnessed this at the abbey when new guests arrived, which was typically right before lunch. There was a five-minute period between when the lunch bell rang and when one of the monks arrived to open the doors to the dining hall and let us in. During the first few days I was there, I felt so naked without my phone during those five minutes. Why? Because almost every newly arrived guest standing there with me was looking at their phone. Not to be rude. Of course not. But only because it was way more comfortable to not be present with strangers in front of them so they could be present with strangers on the internet.

Woof. That'll preach.

How many times do we pull out our phones when we get uncomfortable with our present circumstance? The data is there. I don't even need to quote some Harvard study for you to know it's a problem. We have lost presence. We are no longer *here*. We are only *there*.

Here's a study I did on my own, It's not a peer-reviewed study. It was conducted by the Carlos Whittaker School of Addiction to

Phones. While I was at the Atlanta Hatfield International Airport on a layover, I decided to stand at the top of the Terminal A escalator and count how many people were staring at their phones when they stepped off. For my study to feel scientific, I decided to study one hundred escalator people. And would you like to guess how many of the one hundred people were staring at their phones when they appeared at the top of the escalator? How many of them were looking at the devices in their hands instead of at the escalator stairs disappearing beneath their feet?

If you guessed all one hundred, that's right. You guessed correctly. *Every single human coming up the escalator was looking down at their phone.* You don't have to take my word for it. Next time you are in an airport, do this experiment yourself.

But back to the dining hall lobby with the new guests. Not having a phone in these stranger-danger situations proved hilarious. When I looked people in the eyes and said hello, they typically smiled awkwardly and then went back to looking at their phones while I just looked at them longer. This probably made me a psychopath in their eyes. LOL.[i]

But, man, oh man, did being present 100 percent of the time have its sweet spots. And by sweet, I mean being present legitimately saved my life. Perhaps you're thinking, *Okay, Carlos has now officially gone off the deep end.* No, I'm serious!

Remember the story about how much I love to vacation with my family in New York City? About how it not only forces us to move at God speed by walking but that we also can't really be on our phones? Because walking around the city without being present and paying attention is a sure way to get flattened by a dump truck. Well, it turns out a similar principle applies in the middle of the high desert

---

i. There I go again, typing *LOL*.

of Southern California. On day ten, four days before I was to leave this beautiful oasis—alive, I hoped—I had one of the most present and grounding experiences of my life.

You see, when I drink my first cup of Dunkin' Donuts coffee on my front porch every morning, I watch the sun wake up as well. But by the time I need to start walking down for morning vigils, the sun is still sneaking its way over the mountains to the east. That means it's still somewhat dark out. As you know, there are fifty-seven stone stairs from Mount Carmel to the back of the guesthouse below me. And it's a pretty steep path bordered by rocks, dry bushes, and cacti all the way down.

Once I reach the guesthouse, I make my way through a patio on the right-hand side and onto a path surrounded by green lawn. Literal Psalm 23 vibes. The path takes me through the front lawn of the guesthouse and drops me off by the pond where it forks. I can keep going to the right around the pond to hang out with my duck friends, or I can go left and down more stairs to reach the chapel. Those stairs are set up in groups of five—five stairs, ten feet of path, five more stairs. You get it. The stairs path is surround by evergreen bushes, with a statue of Mary holding baby Jesus halfway down.

Why, you may be wondering, am I painting such a vivid and detailed description of this walk from my cabin down to the chapel? BECAUSE I ALMOST DIED ON THIS PATH! (The all-caps thing was for dramatic effect, so I hope you heard me yelling at you.) And had I been on my phone, I'm certain I would have. *And I need you to be imagining exactly where I was when my life almost ended.*

There I was, minding my own business, enjoying one of my last mornings at the abbey, when I reached the front of the guesthouse and stepped onto the path next to the pond. Something caught my eye to the left, about thirty feet down the path to the chapel. It was sitting right in the middle of the path, but in the dim early morning light I couldn't tell exactly what it was. It looked like it might be one of the abbey dogs that run around and bring an automatic shot of serotonin to my dome.

I didn't even have time to process what I thought it looked like because a split second after I saw it, it gracefully leapt onto one of the side railings along the stairs. When I say *gracefully*, I mean like Natalie Portman in *Black Swan* gracefully. Like Scott Hamilton landing a triple Lutz gracefully. Like Carlos Whittaker stealing a meatball behind Heather's back as she turns around in the kitchen after she told Carlos not to take a meatball gracefully.

I'd thought it was a big dog—maybe the size of my wife's dog, Rome.[ii] Only this was no dog; it moved like a cat. But may I tell you something? *Cats are not supposed to be ninety pounds.* And while I wasn't close enough to weigh this kitty cat, I could tell it was huge. And it was staring at me. Kind of cocking its head left and right. You know, like cats do.

"*No, sir!*" I said. Why I spoke to it as if I were in the military, I'm not sure. "*No, sir!*" I said again. It wasn't moved by my two words. I was stuck. I quickly looked around to see if there was anyone nearby to rescue me from this bobcat standing between me and the chapel. But nope. The only people who show up to 6:00 a.m. vigils are me and the monks, and the monks come from the other side of the chapel. I was alone. I took two aggressive steps toward it, hoping my bravado would startle the cat and it would run away.

Nope.

It just stood there. Still moving its head left and right while staring deep into my soul. I had to come up with a plan. I could try walking to

---

ii. We have two Bernese Mountain Dogs—Hawk and Rome. Hawk is my dog, 130 pounds of confused canine. Cute as a button but just not smart. And then Rome, Heather's version of a Berner, is probably about 90 pounds. I call him a fake Berner because he's so small. Hawk makes Rome look tiny.

the right around the lake and avoid the stairs the bobcat was on in the hope it would just stay where it was. That was plan number one. I was about ten feet from the fork in the path, and the cat was about sixty feet away. I took one single step forward toward the fork and the cat, that freaking cat, matched my step. *It took a step forward toward me.*

"No, sir!" I yelled even louder this time. "*I don't think so!*" But when I took another step forward, *so did the cat.* It. Was. Stalking. Me.

I had seen enough YouTube videos to know this was going to end badly. So I began making an emergency plan. The plan was to straight-up jump into the pond. I mean, cats don't swim, right? *Did I learn that in school or from watching cartoons growing up?* I couldn't remember at that moment, but I knew this was probably my only chance at survival. I scanned the property once again to see if there were any other humans who could rescue me. Still, no one.

Then, before I could take another step, the bobcat got in that position your cat at home gets into right before it pounces on a bug. You know the position. I'm sure people that do yoga know what it's called and do it themselves on yoga mats. It's like a downward dog but more like a crunched cat. It took another step toward me, still staring me straight in the eyes. This was no surprise attack. This cat wanted me to look deep into its eyes before it leapt toward me and sank its fangs deep into my neck. I know I'm being dramatic, but this was what I was feeling!

"Stop it, cat!" I yelled. It took another step. And then another. And another. It jumped off the railing and onto the path before making its way to the next level of path, up five stairs, and then back onto the railing. The cat was now legitimately fifteen feet from me. And I was freaking out.

"*Help! Help!*" I yelled.[iii]

---

iii. Have you ever yelled "help" like that in real life? No? Me neither. Not until I was about to go toe-to-toe with the cat from *Ice Age.*

There was no response to my cries. I looked to my left and saw a large orange traffic cone. It happened so fast I don't even remember grabbing it, but as the cat took another measured step toward me, I picked up that cone and chucked it as hard as I could. I missed the cat by at least twenty feet. *How in the world is my aim that bad?* I never made it past T-ball when I was a kid, and now I know why.

The bobcat watched the cone fly across the path and then turned back toward me. But now it was in a crouched position and wiggling its butt like my cat does right before it pounces. This was it. It was over. I was going to die on the path to the chapel at Saint Andrew's Abbey. What a way to go out.

That's when I noticed that there was one more orange traffic cone about five feet to my left. It was now or never. I took two giant steps to the cone, picked it up, and threw it even harder than the first one. This time that cone barreled straight at the cat's face. It leapt to the right and took off toward the chapel. And I took off across the guesthouse lawn and down the embankment behind it, scrambling down dirt and rocks until I hit the street that the dormitories were on. If someone had filmed me running, I swear I looked like Jason Bourne. But stiffer.

I stopped running because I saw one of the monks. I ran up to him. Out of breath. "Father! Don't go that way! There is a bobcat! It tried to kill me!" That is literally what I said, word for word. The monk started laughing—legitimately laughing.

"Oh, Carlos," he said. "The bobcat wasn't going to kill you. He was probably looking at the ducks behind you."

As soon as he said it, I realized I did remember the ducks squawking and quacking. And they were for sure behind me. Maybe that cat wasn't stalking me after all. Maybe he was looking at me like, "Bro, would you please move? You're blocking the ducks." I don't know. But what I do know is that I must have told that story to other monks and retreat guests ten times that day, and the cat got bigger and my aim with the traffic cone got better every time I told it. By the end of the day, I think my closing line was, "I just can't imagine what might have happened if I had been looking at my phone and walked down the path right into the fangs of the lion."

Luckily for me, I have documentation of the whole near-death encounter for anyone who thinks I might be exaggerating. The fact that I was fearing for my life didn't keep me from pulling out my Sony camera and recording the entire thing.

Did I mention I brought a camera? A camera that takes photos and video but isn't connected to the world? You know they still make those, right? And that would be one of the three things I'd encourage you think about doing to be more present in the world around you.

1. **BUY A POINT-AND-SHOOT CAMERA AND LEAVE YOUR PHONE AT HOME WHEN YOU'RE OUT WITH YOUR FAMILY**. There is nothing better than capturing life's moments so you can remember them and look at them in vivid detail later. However, when our phones are also our cameras, we not only capture the moment, we immediately feel the need to share the moment with people who aren't even in the moment. My point-and-shoot camera is a game changer for me. I am still able to capture moments, but I get to stay in the moment instead of giving the moment away.

2. **GET A DUMB PHONE**. Not only does your wireless carrier still carry flip phones, it's become trendy to use dumb phones again. And dumb phones are making us smarter

while smartphones are making us dumber. Research has shown that smartphones are making us more forgetful and less prone to memorize and learn things because we have the answers always available at our fingertips. I'm not saying you have to get rid of the smartphone—I still have mine! (Obviously, because if you follow me on Instagram, you see me storying all the time.) But you may be someone who needs to split your time between a dumb phone and a smartphone. No shame in that. Dumb phone plus smart camera could equal true presence.

3. **SET CLEAR PHONE BOUNDARIES AND MAKE YOURSELF ACCOUNTABLE**. What use is a boundary you can cross whenever you want? When I told my kids I was no longer going to bring my phone to any table, whether I was out to eat or eating at home, they decided to keep me accountable. And it's been the greatest gift I have given my mealtimes. To be fully present.

Here's a boundary that you can set right now, in this moment, that will literally transform your days. *Turn off notifications.* You know, the thing that kept my monk friend from being fully engaged with me? This is something that I've done that changed the game. I have only three notifications that are allowed to bother me:

i. If one of my family members is calling, my phone notifies me. Not texts. Just calls. If it's a text, they don't need me bad enough in the moment to call.

ii. I let the app BeReal notify me once a day to remind me to take a photo to remember my year.

iii. And last of all, I have a random notification app that reminds me from time to time to *notice*.

That's it. Gone are the email notifications. Gone are the

text message notifications. Gone are the SportsCenter notifications. This simple boundary has allowed me to be much more present.

Another boundary for you to consider: What if you took it a step further and turned your phone on and off like you turn the TV on and off? In our home the TV is never just on in the background. It's on if we are watching something. But when we are done, we turn it off. Try applying this boundary to your phone use. Turn it on when you need it. And turn it off when you don't.

Whatever your boundaries are going to be, make them with the idea that they're going to make you more present and human. You will live more life. I promise.

So, presence. We've lost it. But we can get it back.

Of course, we can remind ourselves of Jesus and his powerful ability to be fully present with those around him. We can take cues from his life and see just how powerful presence can be.

Take the woman at the well (John 4:1–26). Jesus had just shown up in Samaria and was exhausted. So he decided to sit by a well. Samaritans and Jews traditionally had some animosity between them. When a Samaritan woman approached, it would have been easy and understandable in that culture and time for Jesus to avoid engaging with her at any level.

But he broke all social barriers and initiated a conversation with this woman. He asked for a drink. He listened intently and without judgment as she told of her struggles. He absolutely shocked her with his knowledge of her life situation, which was not only a miracle but also an expression of care for what she was going through. And then he offered her living water symbolizing spiritual fulfillment. The woman took off, leaving her water jug, to tell her community about the life-changing conversation she had just had with a *fully present* Jesus.

In fact, Jesus made a habit of being fully present with people that hardly anybody wanted to be present with. His interaction with Zacchaeus the tax collector is another great example. Zacchaeus was up in a tree, looking at Jesus, when Jesus did a very present thing. He looked up into Zacchaeus's eyes and showed him recognition and acceptance. Zacchaeus was probably used to seeing anger and fear in other people's eyes, if they bothered to make eye contact at all. You should read the rest of the story for yourself, but long story short, Jesus' presence with Zacchaeus changed his entire life (Luke 19:1–10). After a career characterized by greed and dishonesty, he ended up pledging to give half of his possessions to the poor and to repay everyone he'd ever cheated.

That is some radical transformation that happened simply because of presence.

Our presence has the ability to change not only our lives but the lives of others. I want some more of *that*, please. That life-changing presence.

So be free of the presence trap that is our phones and their constant notifications. You could change another's life—someone that you might not even notice if you weren't looking up.

Oh, and you can survive a stalking bobcat much better without your phone than with it.

CHAPTER 11

BORED

It's not that the phones are bad," Father Carlos said. "It's just that they keep us from being fully present with each other and with God." No, that wasn't a typo. There was another father there . . . and yes, his name is Carlos. I was riding shotgun with Father Carlos in the abbey truck as we made our way from the ceramics facility back to the main campus. The truck looked like the one that Riggins drove in *Friday Night Lights*. I think it was a Ford F-150. Probably from the 1980s. The seats were weathered and cracked—from baking in the high desert sun at 115 degrees, I'm sure. But it was clean. I mean, it was the Monk Truck. Or as I liked to call it, the Tronk.

Father Carlos had become my friend, and I was sad I would be leaving him tomorrow. He is whimsical and fun but also takes his role as the monk next up to the abbot very seriously. His job at the abbey is managing the ceramics shop. One of the things this abbey is known for is their handmade ceramic angels. People all around the country have them. They ship them worldwide. And it's an entire thing. The ceramics building is gigantic, and Father Carlos runs the whole operation.

I'd been wanting to catch him for a specific conversation about phones and monks because I'd noticed they all had them. Which still weirded me out. But not as much as the fact that Father Carlos asked if he could be my friend on Facebook.

"I love social media," he said. "It has actually helped us sell a lot more ceramic angels. Last year, this TikTok influencer somehow found our ceramic angels and made a video about them. She put up a link to our website, and I think we sold something like $10,000 worth of angels overnight."

I remember mentally removing myself from the truck at that exact moment and not wanting to forget how incredibly surreal that moment felt. I was talking to a monk at a monastery about influential TikTokers while driving around in the Tronk.

"But you know what I think is probably one of the biggest problems these phones are causing?" Father Carlos asked. "People don't know how to be bored anymore. Even the monks. There are some monks who have *phone problems*. Phones are addictive. And I think they are ruining our ability to be bored."

We continued on in an epic conversation about technology and the soul. Much of which I recorded on my Sony camera, so you can be sure I'll be posting that conversation at some point. But the piece about boredom? That stopped me in my tracks. Because it was so true.

It's important to differentiate boredom and solitude. We have already talked about the disappearing art of solitude, but we need to be clear that solitude and boredom are not the same thing.

Boredom is the feeling of not being interested in something or not being stimulated by something. You're bored when you aren't surrounded by activities that are meaningful and engaging, or you're bored simply by being in a situation that is repetitive or monotonous. You end up feeling restless, irritable, and dissatisfied.

Solitude, on the other hand, is simply the state of being alone. It can be a positive thing, which we talked about earlier. A major difference between boredom and solitude is that boredom is a feeling and solitude is a state of being. Boredom means you lack stimulation; solitude means you lack others around you.

When I first got to the abbey, I was bored for sure. I was constantly looking at the clock on the wall of the conference room, watching the seconds tick by and wondering when I would finally be able to leave the most boring place on planet Earth. And look at me now! I am no longer bored, but I am in solitude much of the day. The two can overlap, but they don't have to. You may experience boredom and solitude at the same time, but you can also feel one without the other. For example, if you are at a party, surrounded by tons of people you don't know, you may experience boredom. But if you enjoy spending time alone, you may experience solitude without feeling bored.

It might seem as if solitude is a good thing and boredom is a bad thing, but I don't see it that way. I still got bored at the abbey, but I learned not to run away from it. I just let it take me to places I probably wouldn't otherwise have gone.

I want you to imagine a scenario and answer some questions to gauge where you're at with boredom.

If I grabbed a chair, put it in the middle of a forest, and then sat you in the chair—with no phone, book, or anything else to take your mind off said forest—and I left you there for two hours, how would you do? Is that something you would love? Or would you struggle? The fact is, there are lots of folks who would *love* to spend a few hours alone in a chair in a forest away from the demands of life. And I get it. But I think many more folks would not know what to do. The silence of the forest and the loudness of their mind would be deafening.

Something I do a lot when I'm speaking at corporate events is ask people how comfortable they are with slowing down and lowering the volume of life. Everyone normally shrugs their shoulders as if to say, "Yeah, I'm fine." But then you know what I love to do? In the middle of a sentence, I just stop talking. I say, "Okay, since you all feel like you're good at this solitude thing and you're super comfortable with it, I want to test something out on you. I want to see if you can . . ." And then I stop talking. And people look at each other and then back at me. They probably think I forgot my next line. But then I smile after about fifteen seconds of silence so they don't think I'm a robot that short-circuited. Once they see that I stopped talking on purpose, there is initially relief that nothing is wrong, but then the relief is quickly followed by awkwardness. Because the silence is *loud*. And I stay standing there in complete and total silence for at least a minute. And may I tell you that a minute in silence surrounded by coworkers you are never silent around feels less like a minute and more like an hour?

Then I finally let them off the hook and say, "That was just sixty seconds of silence, and most of you were freaking out."

And it's true. I am nearly blown off the stage by the collective exhale that happens the moment I start talking again. People don't know how to just enjoy the silence, or boredom, of a moment.

I'm not trying to promote boredom as a new wellness movement, but I do want you to think differently about it. Boredom is not something to escape, nor is it something to seek. Rather, since I referred to it as more of a feeling earlier, I want you to think of boredom as an emotion that's worth paying attention to.

Drake Baer, former contributing writer at *Fast Company*, once described smartphones as an endless supply of Cheetos. He says that when we're hungry, we have choices about what we eat. We can eat healthy food or we can eat junk food. Our phones are definitely the Cheetos of boredom. Consuming what they provide may give us a quick hit of satisfaction, but in the long run, we're not doing anything good for our brains or our souls.[1]

Plus, I don't think we realize the untapped potential for creativity and ideas we have when we allow ourselves to be bored. Being bored doesn't have to be, well, boring.

Case in point: In the 1940s, Walter Frederick Morrison and his girlfriend, Lucile, were on a beach in Santa Monica, California. They were bored, so they started throwing a pie tin back and forth. The pie tin flew pretty well, but it was too heavy and could be dangerous. Morrison started experimenting with different materials and designs and eventually came up with the Frisbee, which is now one of the most popular beach toys in the world. The freaking Frisbee was invented out of boredom! Can you imagine if Walter and Lucile had instead spent the afternoon trading TikToks? Then thousands of men in their late thirties would never have been able to play Frisbee golf!

I love TikTok. I scroll and die laughing just like you do. I'm not advocating for the demise of scrolling. But I do want to point out that the lack of boredom in our lives is a problem. If it's a problem for the monks, then it's a problem for us.

Our inability to be bored has ruined our attention spans, which means we no longer have the capacity to focus on one thing for a sustained period of time. If you think that's not such a big deal, consider this. Being a lifeguard requires sustained focus in the midst of a lot of boredom. May I please never see a lifeguard scrolling on their phone while they are on their lifeguard stand. Lifeguards, I know it's probably boring to watch us wade in the ocean for hours and hours on end, *but we need you to stay bored, please and thank you.*

When I was growing up, I always heard the line, "Knowledge is power." But I don't think that's true anymore. Knowledge is no longer scarce; it's readily available to all of us. What's lacking is the ability to stay focused when we're bored. And I believe that being okay with boredom is part of what makes that possible.

———

I want you to think about a moment from the past day or week when boredom began to sneak up on you. What did you do? Did you let it come? Or did you quickly end it by pulling out your phone? Was it in line at the grocery store? Was it waiting in line to pick up your kids from school? Was it in the middle of a meeting when you secretly were watching TikToks instead of paying attention? Now that you see it, how about just letting the boredom come next time? Let it slide into your soul's DMs. Let it hang around awhile. There is so much potential goodness waiting for us inside of boredom.

So how can we begin to foster some healthy boredom in our screen-filled lives?

1. **CREATE SPACE FOR BOREDOM IN YOUR DAY**. Schedule time for solitude and plan to do nothing. Like, I want you to actually place it on your calendar. "Meeting with Solitude from 2:00 to 2:30." When feelings of boredom arise, don't run from them. Just *be*. I know it may be hard for you to just be without doing something or producing something, but give it a try. When you are fifteen minutes into your date with solitude and boredom comes knocking—let it take you where it's gonna take you. Don't start planning the rest of your day or thinking about your task list. Just observe what you're feeling. Sometimes when you let boredom show up

and stay awhile, truly great ideas or new insights will also show up.

There is a saying that "if you're bored, you're boring." That's dumb. How about I make up another saying? "If you are never bored, you're exhausting." There we go.

2. **START BEING A LITTLE BORED AND THEN WORK YOUR WAY UP TO BEING REALLY BORED.** Believe it or not, boredom takes practice. Specifically, *staying* in boredom and not fleeing from it takes practice. So start small, maybe with five minutes. Want to know something weird I did before my two-month experiment? I went into my closet, turned off the light, and sat there for ten minutes. Just to practice being bored. I'm not saying you have to do that, but if you do, make sure you tell someone why you're doing it so they don't think you've lost your mind.

3. **PRACTICE MINDLESSNESS.** Let your mind wander. Don't try to hold it back. If you're one of those people who thrives on being productive, you'll be tempted to try and make this boredom exercise some sort of productivity hack, like mind mapping. But no, it's not. Mindlessness in the sense I'm talking about is letting your mind go to the places that it wants to go. Just follow it.

Sometimes intentional mindlessness can turn into daydreaming. When I was a kid I felt like daydreaming was something to be avoided—like, if I was daydreaming in school I would most definitely get in trouble. But daydreaming can be so healthy and rewarding, a chance for your brain to take a break from problem-solving, focusing on the next thing, or worrying about tomorrow. I'm not saying that we need to stop being productive or responsible. But I am giving you permission to daydream in the midst of your boredom and recognize it for the gift that it is. You never know—you might invent the next Frisbee.

———

Father Carlos and I finished our little interview and stepped out of the truck. "I'm gonna miss you, Father," I said as he walked away. I didn't think he heard me because he didn't reply, and I wasn't going to yell it louder because there were other people around. But when he was fifteen feet down the path, he called back, "I'm going to miss you, too, Carlos! But not as often as you've been missing Mass!"

Busted.

I'm going to miss him for real. But I would miss so much more about my time at the abbey, more than I realized in that moment. I'd learned so much. I wasn't the same person I'd been when I arrived. I'd arrived in a state of stress and panic, and now I was leaving in a state of sweet peace.

In all honesty, the thought of leaving was beginning to bring unforeseen stress to my heart. *Who is going to ring the bells in my life to remind me to pray? How am I going to feel leaving the monastery grounds that I haven't left in two weeks? How am I going to handle seeing my family again? Are they expecting something different than who I have become?*

And the most stressful part wasn't that I was leaving the monastery and moving to an Amish sheep farm. No. It was the in-between that was quickening my pulse. *How am I going to fly from Los Angeles to Cleveland without my Delta app? How am I going to get hold of Lee Ann to pick me up at the airport?* It was going to be like air travel in 1990 all over again.

Paper. I think they still have paper boarding passes.

I made my way back up to Mount Carmel. I wanted the cabin

to be spotless because Heather would be there in just a few hours to join me in my last twenty-four hours at the abbey. If anyone deserved to experience monk Carlos, it was her. This was actually her doing—getting me to come to the monastery where her dad is buried. She'd known many of these monks since she was just a little girl running around the grounds. And she had dealt with her smartphone-addicted husband for fifteen years. The least I could do was give her twenty-four hours of Monklos, the new monk name I'd given myself.

As I swept my tiny kitchen, I began to cry. This version of Carlos was drastically different than the version who had showed up here. I was cringe because I was grateful. Grateful for this opportunity. But also grateful that my wife would be able to live with a new version of me. A version she had probably longed for, for a long time.

A boring version of me.

That was going to be balm to her soul.

Because it already was to mine.

CHAPTER 12
SAVOR

Judy was sitting behind her desk inside the retreat office. There was a heavy iron-bar door that made a really loud clank every time you opened or closed it. Every time I opened that door, I felt like apologizing for the clanking sound. "Sorry to bother you again, Judy. But could you tell me what time it is?" This was the third time in approximately twenty minutes I'd asked her the same question. She didn't miss a beat. "Five minutes since you asked me last," she joked.

But, alas, the seconds seemed to drag on and on.

Anticipating Heather's arrival brought on all sorts of heart palpitations—the good kind. I had *so* much to tell her. So much to catch her up on. And I was assuming she had so much to tell me as well. Not to mention the fact that, as much as I enjoyed monk life, I really enjoyed married life—*all* of it.

I was sitting in the dining hall, expecting Heather to be there by then and really wishing I had Life360 back. Then I finally saw her through the floor-to-ceiling glass windows behind the head monk's table. She kind of skipped when she saw me. I wanted to sprint outside, pick her up, and spin her around at 120 frames per second in super slow-mo, but I knew she would kill me if I tried, so I just waited for her to come in. And when she did, I smiled the biggest smile I'd smiled since I got dropped off. *She's here! In my new world! I can't believe it!*

When she grabbed my hand, I felt like I did when we were first dating. *Crazy!* We sat quietly until the prayer for lunch was over, and then I started talking one hundred miles a minute. She just kept laughing. "You never talk this much. You never talk to me this much. This is amazing!" And it was true. The simple fact that I'd been spending a lot of time without someone readily available to talk to was going to be more and more evident in those next few days. I was about to talk more than I had talked in a long, long time. And Heather was going to be the recipient of this gift.

I'm not going to pretend that we entered a new dimension of our marriage, and I suddenly became the perfect husband. No. I knew I was going to get back on my phone, and I knew we were probably going to get in arguments over it again at some point. But I also wanted to savor this moment. I wanted to savor the feeling that all of us lose when we get too familiar with what we love. If we aren't careful, we can lose our innate and unbridled passion for the very thing that makes our heart skip a beat, whether it's a person or an activity.

For the next twenty-four hours, I did everything I could to savor our moments together. I did everything I could to slow them down. We had the most incredible day together. We hiked to the top of the cemetery so we could visit her dad's grave. We visited the bookstore and then walked up to Bumblebee Lookout. (I named it that because there were always so many bumblebees hopping from flower to flower.) We attended all the hours of prayer. We had silent dinner. We watched the sunset on the front porch. We woke up to the smell of my Mr. Coffee making its Dunkin' Donuts breakfast blend at 5:00 a.m. We did all the things I had grown to love to do every day. I introduced her to all my new friends. I could see in her eyes that she was *really into* this version of me. Now to see if I could keep him around.

The time had come. I packed my bags and dragged them down the fifty-seven stone steps to the driveway that led up to the guesthouse. I threw my bags in the pickup truck Heather had rented, and she drove us over to the ceramics building so I could say goodbye to Father Carlos.

"Now, don't be a stranger, Carlos," Carlos said. (That was fun to type.)

"I won't, I promise. I'm marked for life. I'm Monklos now, remember?"

And with that, I gave him a long hug, climbed into the car, and Heather slowly drove us out of the abbey. I had about two hours to process all that had happened to me before we met up with our kids. They had all flown out to Los Angeles to see me. We were going to have about forty-eight hours of family time before I jumped on a plane to Ohio.

The Amish were waiting.

During the whole drive from the desert to Los Angeles, I couldn't get out of my head just *how enjoyable* the previous twenty-four hours had been. The way Heather and I savored every single moment. Even in my two weeks at the abbey, I hadn't really savored moments the way we had. *Why was that?* I guess savoring is yet another thing most of us no longer do since the advent of smartphones. It's almost like we don't have time to savor anymore.

When I thought about it, I realized that we tend to think more about the things that make us unhappy than the things that make us happy. It's true. We focus on our problems. And it turns out this is a data-backed truth. We worry about our finances, our health, our relationships. But we all want to be happy, right? So why in the world do we spend so much time thinking about what is bad in our lives?

What made the previous day so different was that I didn't think about a single problem in my life for twenty-four hours. I know this is anecdotal and that my entire experiment isn't a scientific experiment because it's based on only one man's experience, but I did make discoveries about savoring that I want share with you. Because if we can get this one thing back, I believe it has the capacity to bring back all the other things we have lost since these phones showed up.

The reason we focus on the hard stuff instead of the happy stuff is because our brains are hardwired to protect us from pain. Which means we are constantly on the lookout for pain so we can beat it to the punch. Hard things hunt after us, but pleasure doesn't. In fact, we have to hunt after it.

Our tendency to focus on the hard stuff as opposed to the happy stuff even reaches into our relationships. For example, consider the fact that much of what we focus on in our parenting is helping our kids to avoid, navigate, or recover from disappointment, pain, or trauma. And that is important. But have you ever thought about teaching your kids how to enjoy a slice of pizza? Of course not. Because that automatically happens if it is a good slice of pizza.

But *enjoying* and *savoring* are not the same. To savor is to *enjoy something completely—with delight and pleasure.* It is to squeeze every last drop of goodness out of it. Mere enjoyment may happen naturally, but savoring is something that has to be learned. We can strengthen our savoring skills in several ways.

First, *be mindful through our focus and attention.* During our brief reunion between the abbey and the Amish farm, Heather and I not only noticed things together but we also intentionally *savored* those things. I'm talking about simple moments and feelings that we usually allow to slip away without taking the time to engage fully. When we watched the sunset, we were filled with gratitude. And we didn't just hop up and go inside. We sat there until it got fully dark. We talked about the beauty of what we'd just witnessed. We recalled other sunsets we had seen together. We savored the moment.

Later I discovered that what we were doing involved a sort of mindful awareness that actually has a name: *metacognition.* That's a fancy word for simply being aware and focusing on the feelings and thoughts we are having at any given moment. This is Savoring 101: noticing, attending to, and appreciating something positive that you experience.

I mean, that's why I was amazed at how good my Dunkin' coffee tasted when I first arrived at the abbey—because I was able to savor it in the morning without reading emails or catching up on social media. It's why the first cup of coffee you have on the first morning of vacation, out of a ceramic mug, tastes so much better than the coffee you knock back from a to-go cup on the way to work.

Savor.

Another facet of savoring is to *stay aware of our instinct to numb to repetition.* It takes work to keep savoring things. Human beings were designed to get used to things, to become familiar with them to the point that we don't have to think about them too much. Otherwise, the perils of the world would overwhelm us. This makes me think about this gigantic tattoo that covers three-fourths of my right arm. Can I tell you how much it hurt? The process of getting a tattoo involves a needle repeatedly being jabbed into your body. And to top it off, I got this tattoo on television, on a show called *LA Ink*, where I had to suffer for four-teen hours of tattooing on camera for the world to see. Fortunately for the world, my segment was edited down to only seven minutes. But oh, the pain!

And yet that experience taught me something about our ability to get used to things. After a while, the pain of the tattoo needles begins to numb a bit. *Numb* may be the wrong word, but my brain began to get used to it. The pain was still there, but I was able to tolerate it more. At the beginning of the process, I was in so much pain that all I could think about was the pain. But three hours into the session, people watching me might not have even realized that getting a tattoo is painful. I was talking to the tattoo artist about my kids and my job, all without hyperventilating (like I was at the beginning). Was the pain still there? Yes. But had I gotten a bit used to it? Yes. Both can be true.

The same dynamic applies to the good stuff. The part of our brain that allows us to become accustomed to the painful parts of our lives also allows us to become accustomed to the sweet experiences. Case in point: the woman I was sitting next to in the car on the way to Los Angeles is the same woman I had said goodbye to a couple weeks prior. But I had gotten used to her before coming to the abbey; I had not practiced savoring.

How about this? You are walking down the street on vacation somewhere, and you feel the joy and bliss of knowing you don't have to do any work for a few days. Suddenly you catch the scent of fresh-baked goods and notice a bakery a few yards ahead. It smells *amazing*! You walk in and are overwhelmed by the aromas of all the sweet and savory carbs stacked up in front of you. You order your croissant, sit at a table, and pull out your phone to scroll TikTok for a few minutes. Every bite is incredible. You are *savoring it*!

A few minutes later, two friends walk into the bakery and they are freaking out about how good it smells. And you suddenly real-ize something. You don't smell it anymore! The smell is gone. Is it because you didn't appreciate it? Of course not. It's simply because you got used to something good in your life. The heavenly aroma was there all along. And you know what you have to do to smell it again? That's right—leave the bakery, walk around the block, and come back in to get hit with the goodness of the smell again.

It's mind-blowing, right? We get so used to the good stuff that we don't savor it anymore.

Another part of savoring requires us to *slow down*. If the idea of savoring still feels a little abstract, it might help to consider what the opposite of savoring looks like. And I can give you a vivid picture of that. Before we had Hawk and Rome, we had another Bernese Mountain Dog named Pope (RIP). One year on Easter, Pope inhaled an entire ham in about ninety seconds. The whole thing. Did that dog savor the ham? Absolutely not. And the truth is, a lot of us are like Pope. We think that by inhaling something quickly, the intense feelings of joy it gives us will bring satisfaction or fulfilment. But every single one of us would do better to savor our moments of joy by making them last a lot longer.

We are moving way too fast through life. So what is the secret to savoring? Well, it's simple. We just have to slow down. It's that God speed thing again. But this time we need to do it for a different reason. This time we do it to savor.

When we were broke during the early years of our family life, Heather and I had a brilliant idea to help make birthday mornings for our kids special even though we didn't have much to spend on gifts. We bought about fifteen two-dollar gifts, wrapped them up, and attached them all to a long string that we ran throughout the house. The birthday kid then had to go gift by gift, section of string by section of string, to slowly open their gifts. *Savoring* them.

Speed and impatience really are the enemy of savoring. The magic is in the lingering.

Finally, we can *guard against comparison.* Comparison takes us out of the moment by measuring what we are feeling or experiencing against what someone else is experiencing, or even what we had anticipated feeling. It goes something like this. You finally get tickets to see the performer you've been wanting to see for a long time. You're at the concert and belting out the lyrics at the top of your lungs, having the time of your life, when you open up your phone to post a photo of you at the show. But before you post, you see that a friend of yours just posted a photo from the same show, only they are sitting on the front row—not way up in the nosebleeds like you are. Suddenly you are comparing experiences and your savoring is over. It's ruined. Because you aren't there anymore. You are sighing and wishing you were somewhere else.

We've all done this, right? We take ourselves out of the moment and go somewhere else instead of savoring. Savoring will always and forever invite us to exist only *in* the moment.

———

Let me explain something to you. You're going to *want* to do what I'm about to lay out for you. Why? Because you will suddenly realize that savoring allows you to squeeze every last drop out of the moment. The simple practices I'm about to describe will allow you to *feel* again. Studies show that savoring can help with our mental health.[1] Also, savoring is going to level up not only *your* life but the lives of those around you. When you savor the moment, the people around you are given the option to join you in savoring. And I've done this enough to know that most of the time, they will join.

So what are ways we can savor the moments that we're given?

1. **ANTICIPATE WHAT YOU'RE GOING TO EXPERIENCE.** When you're looking forward to something, allow yourself to think not just about how great it's going to be, but also about all the incredible feelings you're going have when it happens. Imagine how much joy it is going to bring you. Don't wait to start enjoying what you're looking forward to; savor it before it comes! The intensity with which I look forward to any fly-fishing trip is almost laughable. I savor in advance by researching rivers and streams months before I go.

   Then I imagine it. Feeling the tug at the end of the line and watching my line shoot out from the reel. The sound of wet fly line zipping through the eyelets on the rod. I can literally *feel* the tug. Purposefully anticipating a fly-fishing trip helps me savor it in ways that wouldn't be possible if I just thought about it the day before.

2. **STAY IN THE MOMENT.** Sit longer. Stare longer. Chew slower. Slow down. This is how you can time travel—by slowing down time. You don't have to stop what you're doing to answer your phone when it buzzes. You can check the notification later. One way to stay in the moment is to actually use all your senses. I know this may start to sound a bit over-the-top, but go with me. Sight. Sound. Smell. Touch. Take drinking a freshly poured cup of coffee. Feel the weight of the mug when you pick it up. Don't just start drinking it, but raise the cup up to your nose and smell the coffee. When you finally take a sip, make an effort to consciously think about the temperature of the coffee as you sip. Then let the flavor take over. I just made drinking coffee a full-on drama. There is so much that we miss when we don't savor.

3. **LOOK BACK OFTEN AND CELEBRATE THE MOMENT.** During our two-hour drive to Los Angeles, Heather and I

had so much fun reliving everything we had experienced the day before. We savored it again by celebrating what had already been done. Your enjoyment of a moment isn't over just because the moment is over.

One way to look back and celebrate is to start a savor journal. Once a week you write down not only things that you savored but also the process of savoring them. I think both of these aspects are important—don't just write the moment down but spend some time unpacking it.

For example, I recently pulled out my savor journal and wrote down how I savored a meal at Waffle House with my youngest son, Losiah. It's not just that the waffle tasted amazing. It was also the conversation with my son. Neither of us looked at our phones the entire meal. We laughed about how different our processes were for pouring syrup onto our waffle. (I go square by square and he just pours it on like concrete.) We talked about how much he is looking forward to beginning to drive. And I loved how he looked straight into my eyes as we talked and didn't shift. He was focused. He was savoring it too.

Just writing that out made me savor it *all over again*! And that's the ticket. It's like I had a two-for-one savor moment because I wrote it out.

4. **LOOK FOR BOTH EXTERNAL AND INTERNAL THINGS TO SAVOR**. External things are ones you can savor that are outside of yourself. The way your kid laughs. The thing they say that you don't want to correct because it's so cute, but you know you need to correct because it's going to be awkward when they are twenty-one and still saying "Slipping Booty" instead of "Sleeping Beauty."

And then there are internal things to savor, which are mostly feelings of accomplishment or gratitude. Think about how you feel after a hard workout. You feel sore, but you also feel strong. Savor that. Sit in that feeling longer than you normally would. Savor the accomplishment. Or what about a check arriving in the mail that you didn't know was coming? That is probably a lot easier to savor than a workout! Or when a test comes back negative for something you were worried about? I mean, I will *never* forget the moment Sohaila, my oldest daughter, was in the hospital for what they feared was a horrible disease. You can imagine how it felt when the test results came back negative. Can I tell you that I savored that moment for months? Look for these internal moments of accomplishment or gratitude to savor. We have them on a daily basis. We just have to pay attention.

What about some external things we can savor? Sunsets? Rainbows? Hummingbirds? (Unless you are one of those people who are scared of them. Like me. Sorry, they just sound too much like a bug.) How about savoring a flavor? A friend of mine gave me a rare bottle of whiskey that was aged for twenty-three years. Can I tell you something? When I lift that glass to my lips, I *savor* that sip. I try and squeeze every last bit of flavor out of it. Why? Because it is really expensive, and I know that I won't be able to taste it again until another rare occasion deserves a pour. This is external savoring.

Something else I savored externally at the abbey on a daily basis was a breeze. You can imagine what a breeze does for you on a hot day in the desert. I would close my eyes and feel it fully. It left as quickly as it arrived, but I quickly learned not to miss a single moment of that refreshing breeze. This is savoring, my friends.

It's so hard to savor these days. Especially if you are in the demanding life season that is raising little kids—or, like Heather and me, launching young adults into the world while also taking care of aging parents. The days are long, but the years are short.

Savor them.

I was looking forward to savoring the next forty-eight hours with my kids. I hadn't been around them without a phone in years. Even so, I felt a little bit sorry for them—they were about to get way more of me than they were probably expecting. But that's okay, because then they would be dropping me off at LAX, paper boarding pass in hand, so I could embark on what I'll admit was the part of this experiment I was dreading the most. I may have thought I felt out of place at Monk School, but I hadn't seen anything yet. The chaos that was about to ensue in my life and the lessons I was about to learn were about to take a dramatic turn.

Because in two more days, I was going to Amish School.

PART 2

AMISH SCHOOL

CHAPTER 13

LEE ANN

When was the last time you took a whole trip without your phone? Not a trip to the grocery store. Not a trip to the mall. (Do people still go to the mall?) I'm talking about a trip in a plane, train, or automobile. RIP, John Candy. (Think about it.)

I don't know anyone who still goes to the airport in a taxi they booked by looking up a number in a phone book and calling in a reservation. Nope. We Uber or we Lyft. Which—may I be honest—is amazing. This is yet another reasons why smartphones with apps are a gift: no more yellow pages. I think I saw a meme about this a while back: Growing up, we learned to never get in a car with a stranger we met on the internet—and yet here we are.

Our phone not only makes it possible for us to get a ride to the airport but it also pays for the ride. Our phone has our boarding pass, which means it gets us through security. Once we're past security and seated at our gate, we don't have to call or talk to anyone if we want to change our seat; we can just do it on the airline app. When it's time to board the aircraft, we place our phones on the ticket scanner. When we're buckled in, we connect to the aircraft's Wi-Fi

131

so we can watch YouTube on our phones and text all of our friends and coworkers thirty thousand feet below us on planet Earth. When we land, we use our phones again, either to get an Uber or to text whoever is picking us up. We let them know that we got our bags and are heading out of door B-2. They text us their location when they are getting close, and we text them back to describe what we're wearing so they don't miss us. Then they finally pull up, hop out, give us a hug, throw our bags in the trunk, and we are on our way!

Well, that's the way *you* travel.

That's not the way Amish Carlos travels.

When Heather and the kids dropped me off at LAX, I had two gigantic suitcases—about seventy pounds each—and my backpack and carry-on. I had no phone, so I had to ask the woman at the Delta counter for a paper boarding pass. I held on to that thing for dear life. While walking to my gate, I kept passing these massive screens everywhere. I felt like they were coming at me from every angle, attacking me from all sides. I kept my eyes straight ahead and down to avoid looking at any of them directly. I walked past a sports bar that had a college game on the screen. I wanted to look so bad! But all I kept thinking was, *If I look at these screens, will that mess up my brain scan at the end?!* I didn't want to mess with my little experiment, so I kept staring at the floor.

Walking as fast as I could to my gate, I passed another bar with a TV, and the volume was turned up so loudly I heard a news anchor saying something that would have normally stopped me in my tracks, like a juicy, political steak of a headline. I wanted to stop and watch so bad! But instead, I immediately stuck a finger in my right ear and proceeded to start humming. Not only had I not seen a single screen in just over two weeks, but I had no idea what was happening on planet Earth. I wasn't about to let these evil screens corrupt me!

"Carlos, what are you doing, man?" I said quietly to myself. I was becoming a fanatic in a way I despised in other people. I quickly reminded myself that this wasn't about screens. It was about remembering how we lived without them so we could find better ways of bringing them back into our lives rather than remove them altogether.

I was starting to feel as wound up as I'd been two weeks ago on my flight to Southern California. I needed to put into practice everything I had learned at the monastery. I needed to remember to slow down. To look up. To remind myself, *It's gonna be okay.*

I boarded the plane, pulled out my journal, and started writing.

Well, here we go. I'm already so spun on all of the content I see around me. It's so much. To go from twenty-three hours a day of silence to this is crazy. It's kinda making me a little crazy. I'm not gonna lie. But I just need to breathe and relax and let the day go by. I'll be back to peace and quiet in a few hours.

To be honest, I'm a little worried about how I'm going to be received. Just to put this on paper so I remember what I'm feeling, 2020 was rough on this brother. So many conversations about race that I was leading. So much patience for those that I was trying to teach. So much biting my tongue when people said things that were accidentally racist. It was all so much. And I would be lying if I didn't admit I feel some extra baggage coming with me as I enter this all-white subculture where I am going to stick out like a sore thumb. I'm fairly certain none of these Amish people were deep in cultural conversations about racial reconciliation and such. I guess

I'm just worried that it's going be racist and I'm going to feel judged the entire time. But then again, I *did* sign up for this.

The phrase I always tell the Instafamilia is, "I don't stand on issues, I stand with people." And this is basically that experiment. The Walk with People experiment. It was easier to hang with the monks than it is going to be hanging with the Amish—I'm pretty certain of that. At least I know something about the way Catholics do church and what they believe. I don't even know what the Amish believe. Do they believe in the same God I do? I have no idea. To be honest, all I really know about the Amish is what I learned from horrible reality shows. So I'm sure I am in for a surprise. But this family that is taking me in, they wouldn't be taking me in if they were racist, right? Are there black Amish people? I don't think so. I mean, never say never but that's not something I've seen before.

OMG, I'm getting stressed. Do they have AC? I don't think so. It's so hot in Ohio. It's August. Do I look them in the eye?

Dear Lord, please make the next few weeks fly by. I'm over this.

Looking back at my journal, I realize now how much misinformation I was living under. How much all of the screens that surrounded me had influenced me to form opinions about the Amish that just weren't true. I had let my misunderstandings about them drive fear inside of me.

But there was actually nothing to fear and everything to look forward to. My fear of the Amish was not only unfounded, but the Amish have ended up being some of my favorite people on planet Earth.

And I can't wait to introduce you to them.

I was about an hour from landing in Cleveland. My friend Lee Ann was going to pick me up. She knew what time I was supposed to land and knew I had bags, but I had no way to get hold of her or even know if she was there. *I guess I have to trust the process.*

I looked out the window and just stared. I was bored. Ha! For the first time since I was first at the abbey, I was bored. I missed the monks. I missed the rhythms. I missed the bells. *Do the Amish have bells?* I shut my eyes for a second and the next thing I knew, we had landed.

I walked off the plane and made my way to baggage claim. No sign of Lee Ann. I had her number written down in my journal just in case I needed to borrow someone's phone to call her. *Please don't make me have to do that, Lee Ann.*

I need you to know something about Lee Ann. She is the most opposite of Amish that you could get. Come to think of it, she is the most opposite of a monk that you could get. Lee Ann is a joy bomb. She is a ball of energy just waiting to explode joy on the people around her. Now, I'm not saying that monks and Amish folks aren't joy bombs or energetic; I'm just saying that they aren't near the level Lee Ann is. In addition to being very stylish, she is an incredible designer, a chef who does cooking segments on local TV, and an influencer on Instagram. She's also a dear friend, and I couldn't wait to see her and unload what I'd experienced the last two weeks at the monastery on our drive to Amishville.

Actually, the town is called Mount Hope, Ohio, and it has a population of 190. Yes, that's right—190. Lee Ann lives twenty minutes from Mount Hope in Wooster, Ohio. And Lee Ann is the whole reason I'm here. How is the most opposite-of-Amish person the reason I get to live with the Amish? Because Lee Ann married an Amish man. Only he's not Amish anymore. He left the Amish to marry Lee Ann. That's right. It's a straight-up Amish love scandal.

Lee Ann met her husband, who I'll call D, when she was living with her parents after college. They had an Amish handyman come over to fix something in their home. The Amish man brought his son. Lee Ann took one look at D and told herself she was going to marry that Amish man. Thirty days later, they were married. That's an entire other book that Lee Ann has to write, so I won't get into the specifics, but just know that Lee Ann and D are still tight with D's Amish family. They are all still cool with each other.

I know, I know. Wasn't D supposed to be shunned or all the other stuff that we see on the reality shows? How are they still friends with each other? I don't know for sure, but not only is D still tight with his family after leaving the Amish, he's still tight with the entire Amish community in Mount Hope. D and his best friend, JR, remain best friends even though JR is still Amish and D is not. My Amish scaffolding was already crumbling, and I hadn't even moved in with my family yet.

D is the one who got me in with the family I was going to live with—the Miller family. All I knew was that they were farmers and they had agreed to let this author come and live with them to experience as much of the Amish life as he could in two weeks. And this was only after I had been rejected by numerous other families.

I'll be honest. My people-pleasing tender heart still got its feelings hurt knowing that so many had downright rejected me. I even drove up to Holmes County (where I was going to be living) and asked a family face-to-face if I could move in with them. They initially said yes, and then they changed their minds. So this Miller family was sort of a last-second switch. Lee Ann didn't know much about them either. So I was kind of going in blind. And so was she.

"*Carlos!* Hey, you look like a monk. Do you feel like a monk? Oh my goodness, you have to tell me all about it! My Beetle is parked illegally outside, but I told the man on the sidewalk to watch it real quick. Do you have your bags? *Carlos!* It's so good to see you!"

Lee Ann had arrived.

We got my bags and walked outside where she had illegally parked her comfortable white Beetle. Not a care in the world. I threw my two gigantic suitcases in her backseat, because that thing ain't got no trunk, and climbed in.

"Okay, Carlos. You have to catch me up. Seriously. I want to hear all about it. We have about three hours until we drop you off at the farm. Do you need anything? Do we need to go to the grocery store? Are you going to want to eat with them every meal? Do you have food? What do you need, Carlos?"

There were too many questions flying into my ears, and I didn't have answers to anything. I was just as confused as she was. All I really wanted to know was if I was going to have to sleep in a barn next to animals or if I had a bedroom somewhere. I was a simple man now. I didn't know how to answer her questions with anything but, "I don't know, Lee Ann. You are in charge. Just get me to where I need to be and know I'm so grateful for you. May I tell you about the monks?"

"You absolutely can, Carlitos!" she said. "But maybe in, like, four minutes? We have to start your Ohio Amish adventure with this song." And then with the top down, she cranked up Taylor Swift's "Shake It Off" on her speakers and sped off. Like, pedal to the metal sped off. We were on our way now. Boppin' to TSwift and heading straight to a four-way stop in the middle of Amish country.

My Amish adventure could not be starting off in a more non-Amish way. And I loved it. I was savoring it. What a gift this woman was in my life. I was so grateful for her. We hit the freeway with the top down and speakers blaring. Not a single word was uttered about the monks or the monastery. But we did scream Taylor Swift lyrics at the top of our lungs. I felt so alive. We sped toward Mount Hope, Ohio. That poor town was about to meet its match. Me, Lee Ann, Swift, and her convertible Beetle. *Amish school* was about to commence.

CHAPTER 14
THE MILLERS

My heart was in my throat as we pulled into the Millers' long gravel driveway, about a mile from the four-way stop in the center of town. The driveway ran about fifty yards back behind the farmhouse on our right. To the left was a field, and farther along the driveway was the biggest barn I'd ever seen. Kind of like if Costco sold barns. It was filled with rolls of hay.[i]

Lee Ann turned down the music as we drove past the farmhouse and down the driveway. When we rounded the bend, I saw a young woman standing in the driveway with one hand on her hip and the other waving us down. Behind her was a gigantic field with an Amish woman standing on some sort of plow behind four huge horses. The horses weren't moving. Then from around the other side of the horses an Amish man appeared and yelled, "Gee! Gee!" and the horses started moving. He started making his way over to where Lee Ann and I had parked, while the woman behind the horses, whom I assumed was his wife, took off, hanging on to the reins

---

i. Rolls of hay are apparently more commonly known as *round bales* or just *bales* of hay. The things you learn being Amish . . .

while whatever large farming equipment she was standing on did what it was supposed to do.

The young woman in the driveway was the first to greet us. "You must be Carlos!" she said with a huge grin on her face. I assumed there weren't a lot of Carloses who lived around here, especially who also matched the description she'd been given.

She looked like she was in her late twenties, wearing a denim button-up shirt, jeans, and boots. Her hair was in a ponytail, and freckles sprinkled her cheeks. She had one of those faces that seems to smile even when she wasn't smiling. Just a delight of a human.

"Yup! That's me," I said. "And what's your name?"

"I'm Christa. I'm Willis's youngest daughter, and I run the tiny house you'll be staying in back behind the old barn."

Cue dramatic music playing in my brain to celebrate that I would be living in a tiny house and not the barn.

"That woman over there driving the horses, that's my mom, Kathy," Christa continued. "And over there in the barn pulling hay bales, that's my brother, Timmy. But he likes Tim now that he's older. And here comes my daddy, Willis."

As Willis approached, I gave him a solid look-over. He was the quintessential Amish man I had imagined—about five feet nine, wearing blue work pants and suspenders over a denim shirt. He had a really cool, fully brimmed strawish hat (I say *strawish* 'cause I don't know if it was really made out of straw, but it looked like it was) and a thick yet neatly trimmed white beard—sans the mustache. He was built like you might imagine a farmer would be built. At least, how I would imagine. Kind of like he could be a wrestler if the farming thing didn't work out.

"Hello there," he said with a smile. "You must be Carlos. I'm Willis. Welcome to the Miller Sheep Farm." He stuck out his hand to shake mine. I felt like I was shaking hands with a man who had done more physical labor in the last five hours than I had done in my entire life. His fingers were thick and calloused. His grip was firm, but thankfully he didn't squeeze hard enough to make me wince, and he looked me square in the eye when he spoke.

"Hello, Willis," I said. "First of all, thank you so much for the hospitality. I promise I will try to stay out of your way and be as respectful as possible of your way of life. I know this is probably not normal—"

He cut me off. "This ain't a museum, Carlos. Let's get you to work." He said the last words as he turned and started walking away. *I guess I'm supposed to follow him?* I hadn't even changed yet. I had packed "farm clothes" I was going to put on, but alas, I guess we didn't have time for that.

As I turned to follow Willis to the barn, I saw Lee Ann dying of laughter as she recorded me walking away on her phone.

"See you later, Carlos!" she called out. "I'll be back to check on you in a few days!" Then she got in her white convertible Beetle and zipped off.

"I'll take your bags to the tiny house, Carlos," said Christa. "They'll be there when you and Dad are finished."

When I caught up to Willis, he pointed to something metal-looking in the grass and said, "Could you grab the end of this bar while I grab the other end, and help me carry it over to the tractor?" I picked up one end of some large, dirty, greasy thing, and tried to hold on with every ounce of non-blue-collar strength that I had. I was able to carry my end, but only out of sheer, stubborn determination not to be embarrassed by the first task I had been given.

"Thank you, Carlos," Willis said. "Hop on the Gator and let me give you a tour."

We hopped on his ATV, and I need to let you know that I was already getting confused. *How were we driving around in an ATV if* the Amish don't drive cars? Why did he have horses pulling a plow if he could just strap the plow to the back of the ATV? So many questions.

Willis started driving me around the most beautiful Amish farm I'd ever seen. Now, understand that this may have been one of the only Amish farms I'd ever seen, but it was stunning. When we headed down the driveway toward the back of the property and past the field that Kathy was working on, the land opened up into beautiful, rolling pastures that continued for acres and acres before hitting a tree line.

As we came over a bluff, I saw the cutest tiny red home.

"That's the Poppy House," Willis said. "That's where you'll be staying."

All I knew was that I saw an AC unit sticking out the back of one of the walls, and I shed a tear of gratitude and relief that I wasn't going to bake inside it. *Thank you, Lord, that these Amish have AC. But is that allowed?*

Directly in front of the Poppy House was a pasture with five sheep, three of which were lambs stumbling around and chasing each other. *They're so cute!* We kept heading down the path, and then Willis stopped and had me hop out to open one of the gates so we could get the ATV through it. The gate was one of the large cattle gates you see in all the movies. And even this job was a bit more complicated than I thought. I had to kind of lift it and carry it—it didn't swing. I don't know why, but something about even opening the gate for him made me feel like a hardworking farmer. Like, I may as well go ahead and retire from authoring because I know how to carry heavy things and open gates now. I was basically a farmer.

Willis spent the next hour driving me all around the property. Every corner had a story. There were sheep everywhere. Hundreds of them. And he had some horses too. He pointed out a house in the middle of one of the fields that he rents to his cousin's family. Then we drove past Kathy and the plow, and she waved a gigantic wave and smiled. She looked like she was enjoying driving those horses. We headed back to the main house, and I noticed a smaller house about twenty yards away.

"Who lives there?" I asked.

"Oh, that's my father's house," Willis said. "He's lived on this farm since he was born. His father bought the farm in the early 1900s. He was born here, I was born here, and my kids were born here." Man, just the lineage part of this farm was already inspiring me.

"Does he still help with the farming?" I asked.

"Last year was his last year cutting the hay," Willis said. "He just can't stand behind the horses too long anymore. But I still find him standing in the middle of the field early in the morning checking on the grass. And he still gives me intel as to what he thinks the weather is gonna do. So he's still enjoying life."

We rounded the corner and headed back toward the barn. "Let's go check on the sick pen," Willis said. We went into a smaller barn and there were a few sheep lying down.

"I've got to give them their antibiotics, and I'm gonna need some help," Willis said.

What? I've literally been here two hours and now I'm a vet? What is happening?

Willis told me to move behind the sheep and try to guide them into this sort of tunnel where he would grab them, check their eyes, and give them their meds. I need you to go ahead and play some sort of comedic music in the background as you imagine the chaos of me trying to convince the little sheep to obey my directions. I would come up behind the sheep, and they would take off the other direction.

"Let's go, little sheep!" I said. "Mr. Willis wants to make you better! C'mon, you got this." I had abandoned all semblance of pride and was talking in a baby voice to these sheep in front of their very tough and macho shepherd.

I'd run left and the sheep would run right. I'd go right and they would go left.

"Here, use my staff," Willis said, and he pointed to his freaking *shepherd staff*. Like the one Charlton Heston held at the top of Mount Sinai when he played Moses in *The Ten Commandments*!

"Just tap them with the staff and they should listen better," he said.

So with Willis's coaching and a few failed attempts at using his Moses staff, I eventually guided the sheep into the pen. Willis gave them their meds and then let them back out. After two hours of shadowing this sheep farmer, I was exhausted.

"Why don't you head to the Poppy House, clean up, and meet us for dinner in an hour," Willis said. "I've got a lot of my family coming over. They want to meet you. My brother and his family, and then my grandkids and my other daughter and her husband. And maybe a few more."

I had already had more conversation in the last three hours with Willis than I'd had with anyone the entire time I was at the monastery. My mouth was actually tired from talking! And my brain was tired too. Becoming a professional farmer and a professional vet all in one day will wear you out.

"Okay, thanks," I said. "This is going to be amazing. I'm so grateful." Then I walked out of the sheep pen and onto the gravel road that would lead me back to the Poppy House. As I walked, I kept thinking how freaking blessed I was to be able to do this. I was also thinking how freaking exhausted I was. And I hadn't really done anything!

When I got to the Poppy House, I stood there in awe, just soaking it in. There was a ladder immediately to my left that led up to the loft where the bed was. I climbed up to look and noticed that the ceiling was so low I'd barely be able to sit up in bed, but it looked perfect for sleeping. There was also a lamp and windows that looked out over the pasture.

Back on the main floor, there was a kitchen with a sink and stove to the right and a counter space with bar stools to the left. Keep walking straight and there was the bathroom with a shower. To the right of the front door was a little nook with a sort of sofa built into it. Three walls of that side of the tiny house had seating. Almost a U-shaped sofa. And that was it. The Poppy House was about one-quarter the size of what I'd had at the monastery, but it was perfect—because there was electricity and AC.

I found my way to the sofa and lay down. It didn't take but half a second before I was sawing logs. Completely out like a light.

Then I was suddenly awakened by a knock on the front door.

"Dinner is ready, Carlos. Everyone is waiting to meet you!" Christa said. "I'll wait out here for ya."

I mean *wow*! I legit had drool still leaking from the side of my mouth. That deep-sleep drool that happens only after a week away at camp. That exhausted drool.

"Okay! Be right out!" I said with an excitement that could only be described as a flat-out lie. I was *tanked*. But I walked over to the sink and splashed cold water on my face, slapped myself a few times, took a deep breath, and headed out the front door.

"Now you are gonna meet my niece and nephew," Christa said. "My nephew's a handful, but I promise you will love them both. He's been looking forward to meeting you."

On our five-minute walk back to the main house, she gave me the lowdown on the family. Yesterday when Lee Ann and I had pulled into the driveway, the first thing I'd noticed was that Christa wasn't wearing the kind of clothing I thought she would be wearing.

Like, I assumed she would be wearing a long, simple dress and a bonnet. So the modern clothing was a bit confusing. And I noticed her brother didn't have Amish clothes on either; Tim was wearing blue jeans, a button-up shirt that looked like it was from The Gap, and Nike tennis shoes.

But as we approached the family, Christa's sister looked *very* Amish. Her hair was up in a bun and she had on very simple yet beautiful clothes—a long dress with sleeves that went three-fourths of the way down her arms. And her nephew, Lane—who proceeded to run straight toward me and lunge with the full expectation that I would catch him—was wearing the cutest little homemade Amish outfit ever. You could tell it was a homemade pair of overalls with the biggest buttons on the straps. He even had a little mini version of the straw hat that Willis was wearing when I met him.

"Chase me!" Lane commanded. May I tell you what I wanted to do the least on planet Earth at that moment? Chase after a four-year-old Amish boy. Nothing inside of me had the capacity to do that. "Chase me, mister!" Lane commanded again. Christa saved me.

"Carlos has had a long day, Lane. Let's let him meet everybody first, okay?" The boy took off around the house at lightning speed. When and if I ever do try and chase him, I will fail. Miserably.

Everyone was sitting around a large fire pit, and one by one the family members introduced themselves. First I met Kathy, Willis's wife, the one who'd been driving the horses all afternoon. Imagine Lee Ann's bigger-than-life personality but Amish. She was full of zest, spritely, and really talkative.

Then Christa's brother, Timmy. Tall. Athletic. A lot quieter than his mom. Didn't look like what I thought a young Amish man would look like. Kind of like his sister in the sense that he wasn't wearing traditional Amish clothing. And I met his fiancée, Brenda. Her clothing looked more Amish than Christa's, but not all the way. Not what

I was beginning to think of as *full Amish*. Kinda like a mix of Christa and her mom. Her hair was in a bun like the rest of the Amish women I had seen, but she had more color poppin' in her outfit.

Then I met Tim and Christa's sister, Diane. *Full Amish*. Those were her kids running around. And I met Diane's husband, Ed. *Full Amish*. He had the hat on and everything. Willis's brother and his family were there as well. *Full Amish*-looking.

When I write that I was thinking things like "Amish looking," you've got to remember that I was navigating this entirely new culture blind. I had no idea about anything. And I didn't know if I could ask. I didn't know what was rude. Like, there were cars in the driveway, and right next to the cars was a horse and buggy. *What is happening here?*

"So I have questions," I whispered to Christa. She laughed out loud and said to everyone, "Carlos has questions! Well, *so do we!*" Everyone got a kick out of that, and it felt like permission to just be dumb.

"So are you all Amish?" I asked. "I'm confused."

"Okay, so Mom and Dad are Amish," Christa chimed in. "You can tell. Timmy and I both left the church last year. We are Mennonite. Diane and her husband and kids—all Amish. My dad's brother and all his other siblings—all Amish. Well, except for Uncle Gerry. He's not Amish."

I was shook. Didn't they shun and banish kids for leaving the Amish here like they do on the reality shows?

"Okay, um. I think I get it," I said.

Christa jumped back in. "You probably just know what you know from TV. That's okay. There's gonna be a lot you are gonna have to unlearn so you can learn it right. We are all open books. Mom and Dad are amazing, and any of us will answer any questions you may have. Anytime. No worries."

Wow. So non-Amish family members are living with Amish family members. This was all too much for me to get my head around, so I just kind of gave in and chatted around the campfire for what seemed like hours. I didn't have a watch and there were no monastery bells, so I was kinda screwed.

"Well, we best be getting home," Diane said. "Carlos has his first big day of farming tomorrow! He should get some shut-eye." Everyone laughed. I didn't know what time it was, but I knew it felt as if I had moved from a cave in the middle of nowhere to New York City in one day. The Amish *go hard*. When I got back to my tiny house, I checked the clock. *It was 10:00 p.m.!* We had been talking around that campfire for four hours!

This was an entirely new rhythm for me and, honestly, it was a bit of a shock. Four hours eating and talking around a campfire. And I was told to be ready to meet Willis at 6:30 a.m. for breakfast before we hit the fields.

How was monk Carlos ever going to survive this pace of life? They go nonstop! *Lord, give me strength. It's going to be quite embarrassing when I pass out in the middle of the field tomorrow right in front of Willis.*

I turned off my light at 10:15 p.m. I was asleep by 10:15 and one second.

The Amish wore me out. And it was only day one.

CHAPTER 15

THE TABLE

I t felt like the alarm went off the second after I closed my eyes. I don't think I moved at all in the eight hours I was asleep. More drool. To avoid hitting my head on the loft ceiling, I slid my way to the foot of the bed and awkwardly tried to maneuver down the ladder to the main level. Let me tell you, I am already not a flexible man. And to get up super stiff after a night's sleep and try to descend that ladder barefoot was a sight to behold. I put on my farm clothes and headed out. I knocked on the front door of the farmhouse at 6:29 a.m.

"C'mon in! Have a seat," Willis said as he grabbed me a mug. "Coffee?"

"Yes, please," I begged.

Kathy was in the kitchen making something that smelled amazing. Willis brought me the coffee and a newspaper.

"This is our Amish paper," he said. "It's kinda like Amish Facebook. It has all the information on the community that you would need to know. Who needs help. Who died. Who was born. Who is selling what. Have a gander," he said as he tossed the paper in front of me. I perused it for a few minutes, and then Kathy brought breakfast over and we ate and chatted for what had to be thirty minutes. That was twenty-six minutes longer than breakfast normally takes me to eat at home. And when it was over, Willis leaned back in his chair, took a couple deep breaths, and started planning our day.

We were going to try to cut hay before noon. "Looks like it may rain, so maybe we won't cut it till tomorrow," Willis said. Apparently, you can't cut hay and then have it rain on the cut hay. Makes it bad. After cutting hay, we would head to the livestock auction to see if there were any lambs he wanted to bid on. But it was going take a bit to get there because, well, no cars and stuff. Willis and his family used bikes and horse-drawn buggies to get where they needed to go.

After the auction we were going to have lunch with JR, Tim's best friend, who owns the furniture store. After lunch we'd come back to the farm to check on the sheep for a few hours. Then we'd need to fix a wheel on the ATV that was going bad. Finally we'd have dinner with Doddy (this is what they called Willis's dad) and possibly Tim's fiancée, Brenda, would join us as well. The day was *slammed*. I was getting tired just listening to him plan.

I'd been with my Amish friends for less than twenty-four hours, and already I'd discovered yet another thing we've lost as a society. We've forgotten how to have meals. Like, true meals together. I had eaten two meals with them—dinner the previous night had lasted four hours, and breakfast this morning had lasted forty-five minutes. We were at a table. The meals were cooked at home. We took our time eating them. And lunch that day would end up being about ninety minutes. The Amish did not play around when it came to meals.

The topic of meals came up recently when I interviewed professor and therapist Dan Allender on my podcast. He said that the average American meal today lasts about twelve minutes. *Twelve minutes.* That was shocking to me. And then he said that one hundred years ago, the average American meal lasted approximately ninety minutes.[1] An hour and a half. We no longer have meals like they were meant to be had. I mean, we eat. But do we really have a meal?

The table is one of the most intimate settings we have for sharing our lives. The act of eating together is itself an intimate experience. The table is where we share stories with each other about our days. It's also where we can have crucial conversations about the state of the world. But instead we share our lives and have those crucial conversations online. And would you please tell me how that is going for you?

The table is one of the best tools we have to get to know someone well—to discover the heart of somebody. Getting to the depths of someone's story takes time and care, and the table is one of the safest spaces to begin that process—especially if you're doing the labor of trying to understand someone you disagree with. I've had many of those conversations over the years, and I often had them over a meal. Because you know what the table offers? It offers the opportunity to meet and work together on things we disagree about while simultaneously enjoying something we do agree about—good food! Trust me, if we start a difficult conversation while sharing food we both love, we're already starting from a more unified place than if we'd had the conversation elsewhere.

Why in the world do we think that text messages or even phone calls are any way to approach the depths of the human heart? They aren't! And so, the table. This is what we have to get back to.

After our ninety-minute lunch, I straight-up said to Willis, "You guys take a long time to eat! I'm not complaining. I'm just wondering why."

"I guess the question itself begs another question," Willis said. (Seriously! It's like he's the Amish Yoda.) "The question I'd ask you back is, What actually is a long time? Maybe you take way too short of a time to eat, and we are taking the correct time. If that is the case, then we don't take a long time."

I guess he was right. I was asking the wrong question. The question I needed to be asking was, Why are we taking so little time around the table? And the answers to that question are both simple and haunting.

To start, we speed though meals because we live such busy lives. We eat on the go, or we slam down our meals in minutes, or we skip meals completely. In general, our lifestyles don't allow us to slow down enough to have a meal of thirty minutes. I laugh even thinking about telling my teenagers that dinner tonight is going to last ninety minutes, and no one is leaving the table until it's over. They. Would. Die. Why? Because it feels like a waste of time. But it's not. It's actually doing a few things for us.

Sharing meals together literally reduces our stress. When we eat too fast, it creates stress in our digestive system. And stress hormones can lead to weight gain and all sorts of other health problems. Plus, our bodies don't have enough time to absorb all the nutrients from our food. This can lead to nutrient deficiencies and still other health problems.[2] I'm starting to sound like some nutrition influencer! But no, that's not my point. I'm just trying to explain that not only is the speed at which we consume our meals bad for society in general, it's also bad for our bodies.

According to a study by National Public Radio, the Robert Wood Johnson Foundation, and Harvard University health researchers,

"Almost one in two families are struggling to find time to dine together . . . 46 percent said it was difficult to eat together on a regular basis, and fewer than half of the parents said their family had eaten together six nights in the past week." Researchers also found that the frequency of family dinners has gone down by 33 percent in the last two decades alone, and even when families do eat together it's often in front of a television screen."[3]

I think we all get it. I think we can all feel it. When it comes to meals, we all know that we are too distracted to actually enjoy the miracle that a meal actually is. At the very least, can I recommend that we stop bringing the phones to the table? And maybe don't get up as soon as the meal is over—that's a prime opportunity for building real community and connection. You could even try having multiple courses instead of one quick plate. There are lots of options here, but I want to challenge you to think about it: What are things that you can do today that will bring back the beauty of what a meal is supposed to be?

One thing I noticed pretty quickly with the Amish and their long meals was that meal prep was a family affair. Believe it or not, it wasn't just the woman in the kitchen slaving away. The men were involved in the cooking. The kids were involved in the cooking. It was a family task. Everybody joined in. And when everyone joins in on making something, more often than not, you end up savoring it a little more. Why? Because *you made it*. You did that. And when you make something instead of something being made for you, you end up taking care of it and admiring it a lot longer.

My family has a holiday tradition we started when the kids were little—we make homemade pasta on Christmas Eve. The first time we did it, Seanna (six years old at the time) and I were in charge of making the pasta. Heather, Sohaila (eight), and Losiah (four) were in charge of the pasta sauce. Can I tell you how absolutely horrible the first batch of pasta was that Seanna and I made? We may as well have been eating Play-Doh. It was so bad. But we acted like it was from some Michelin Star restaurant. Everybody complimented it. Everybody ate slowly. Because we were savoring not only the flavor of this horrible pasta but also the hard work that went into creating the pasta.

Let me also tell you that all these years later our pasta is award winning. Well, not real-life award winning, but Seanna and I give ourselves an award every year because our pasta is *so good*! And the meal is an experience—much more than just a time to satisfy hunger.

You may not make homemade pasta as a family, but you know what I'm talking about, don't you? We all went through the pandemic together. Family mealtimes increased 20 percent during the pandemic. Why? Because we had *nowhere to go*. And so many of us collectively rediscovered that homemade family meals enjoyed together are just better.

There is so much data now about the benefits of family meals shared together. And if you are single, having meals with friends counts too! Here are just a couple of tidbits from recent research.

According to survey results from the American Heart Association, 91 percent of parents noticed their family was less stressed when they shared family meals together.[4]

A recent study published by *Dialogues in Health* found that for girls, a "better family meal environment quality at age six predicted an earlier bedtime, a lower consumption of soft drinks and sweet snacks, more classroom engagement, and fewer behavior problems at age twelve."[5]

Even without the data, I don't think I have to work too hard to convince you that the Amish are doing something right, and most of us are doing something wrong. So what do we do? Here are a few things we have begun to implement as a family because of what I learned about meals from my time with the Amish.

1. **EVERYBODY HELPS WITH THE COOKING.** This isn't something that happens every single day, but I'd say more times than not we are all working in the kitchen in some way, shape, or form to prepare the meal. From setting the table to peeling the potatoes to washing the pots as we use them— even if it's something simple, your kids can pull this off. I saw seven-year-old Amish boys driving their toddler sisters around in horse-drawn buggies. You can trust your kid to wash the lettuce.

2. **NO TECH AT THE TABLE.** Seriously. No phones, no TV, no nothing. And keep them out of the kitchen or dining room while you're eating. In other words, no, you may not put your phone on silent and keep it in your pocket. That goes for Mom and Dad too. It's actually harder than you might think. But it's worth it. I'm not saying you can't ever enjoy pizza and a movie, but don't make that normal. Start making it normal that there is no tech at the table. I even try to put away my phone when I'm eating alone on the road. If you are bored, then you need to eat better food.

3. **EAT AT THE TABLE.** That's right. Make the table the centerpiece. No sofa eating. No counter eating. Eat at the table. And if you don't have a table, save up and buy one. Our table used to be the catch-all for backpacks and mail and such. We try our best to not let that happen so the table remains a little sacred. And a card table works just as well as a fancy oak table.

4. **SCHEDULE DINNER**. Legit. Don't just let it happen. This is something the Amish do so well. Dinner was always at 6:30. And if Kathy needed help, we knew what time to be there. That way, we scheduled our day around the meals as opposed to our meals around the day. Same with breakfast. Willis knew what time each meal was and how long it would last, and he arranged our daily tasks around them.

I know how hard it may seem to do these things, but I also know how important it is to do them. Amazing things can happen at the table, including healing. Just having your kids see your eyes on them—rather than your phone—for thirty minutes a day while they are eating will give them an anchor. Just adding minutes opens the meal up to pulling out conversations from your family members that you may not expect. And to be honest, it will feel awkward at first. It will. We are so used to getting up and leaving the table as soon as we take that last bite. But push back against that habit. Let the awkward silence reign for a while. Don't feel like you have to fill up every moment with a question. Just sitting together in silence is okay. You are all thinking things. At some point those individual thoughts will turn into conversations together. You got this.

"Willis, do you eat like this every day? How are you not five thousand pounds? I've only had two meals here and I feel like I've gained twenty pounds," I said after breakfast as we were on our way to the fields.

"Oh, Carlos," he said with a knowing smile, "you are about to feel how we keep the weight off."

I used to do CrossFit. I paid over $200 a month so I could go to a gym and do the exact thing that Willis had me do for the next three hours. At the gym we held heavy kettlebells in each hand and walked back and forth five times with the simple goal of not dropping them. The move was called "farmer's carry." I had to laugh when I realized Willis did CrossFit every day and it didn't cost him a thing. Because that's just what farmers carry.

I squatted, I cleaned and jerked, I deadlifted. I jogged. I walked. I probably did six CrossFit workouts in the three hours before lunch. Not only was I not going to gain any weight, I began to think I might end up looking more like the fine specimen my wife hoped I would become in my late forties (as opposed to the dadbod she got).

The day was long. I guess I can stop saying that now because every day was long. Just plug that into everything I say from here on out. The days were so long that every night around 9:00 p.m. we sat around the patio table and Kathy poured us all coffee like it was 6:00 a.m. And we would all drink coffee. The Amish love coffee. And they drink it all day. I used to stop drinking coffee by 11:00 a.m. or it would keep me up all night. But not Amish Carlos. Amish Carlos was so wiped at the end of every day that 9:00 p.m. coffee had zero effect on how fast I fell asleep.

I got back to the tiny house that night and saw my journal lying on the couch. At the monastery I had written in that thing multiple times a day every single day, but I had yet to pick it up since I'd been here.

"Sorry, little journal," I said. "I don't think I'm gonna have much time for you while I'm here." I'm not sure why I talked to it other than the fact that it looked lonely. So I picked it up and started reading my previous entries, which made me a little homesick for the abbey. I missed the bells. I missed the vespers. I missed the monks. I missed the calm. I missed the silence. I missed the rhythm.

I grabbed a pen and willed myself to write something, which turned out to be just twenty-four words:

It's night two. The Amish are nice. I'm exhausted. I can't decide if I want to be a sheep farmer or a monk. Goodnight.

Wow. I was almost embarrassed. *That's all I have?* Tomorrow was Sunday, so I was going to have a day off from farming. Christa had invited me to go to church with her and Timmy. They went to a Mennonite Church. I wasn't sure if I was even allowed to go to the Amish church with Willis and Kathy. It seemed like what happens in the Amish church is kept low-key and only for those in the community. And to be honest, I already felt like a fish out of water. In a small town where everybody knows everybody, it felt like I had a spotlight on me everywhere we went. People smiled when they stared but they stared nonetheless.

Christa and Willis had filled me in a bit on what Amish church services were like, and if I'm being honest, Amish church sounded like something I wasn't gonna necessarily love. Take me to the good old progressive Mennonite Church instead! I laughed at the thought of how *progressive* and *conservative* in this culture meant something totally different than they did back in my world.

I rolled over to look out the window and saw the little lambs sleeping curled next to each other. All the sheep in the pasture had moved right next to the tiny house. I thought I would literally count sheep until I fell asleep. This was going to be fun.

One, zzzz.

CHAPTER 16

GET LOST

Sunday morning I made my way down the path from the tiny house to the main farmhouse around 7:45 a.m. I saw Willis over at the barn brushing his horse. His sleek black buggy was nearby. I'd never seen a horse buggy up close before. This thing was sharp. It even had turn signals. The inside was straight-up leather. I mean, this seemed like the Tesla of Amish buggies.

"Good morning," Willis said. "How did you sleep?"

"I tried counting the sheep in the pasture outside the window," I said. "And wouldn't you know it, they put me to sleep!" There we were. Two dads standing next to a horse and buggy, laughing over dad jokes.

"Are you going to church this morning too?" I asked. "Where is your church located?"

"Oh, our church is all over," he said. "Our boundary extends from the east side of Highway 34 until it hits Westside Road by the Yoder Farm and then stretches south a good bit."

I wasn't sure he understood my question. "No, like where is your church—the building where you have church?"

"Oh, I see what you are asking," he said. "We don't have a church building. It's called the barn!" He chuckled at his own answer. "We don't have a building like you do or like Christa does. We meet in each other's barns and rotate who is hosting church every other Sunday. So with the amount of families in the church, we will host church in our barn twice a year. All the members of the church will come to our farm, and we will have church here!"

"Whoa, that's amazing!" I replied.

"Yeah, it's the way it's always been," Willis said. "And this is probably a little different than the way you do it as well. We don't have church every single week. We only have church every other week. That way we can visit other churches. This week our church isn't gathering, so all of us will go visit another church. Every week you have lots of visitors at your church because of all the churches that are not meeting that week. This week, Kathy and I are going to visit my cousin's church. Make sense?"

I mean, sort of. I kind of loved that idea. They only meet with each other half the year and the other half they are out and visiting other churches. What a concept!

"I think Kathy has some breakfast ready for you if you want it," Willis said. "I'll be there in a few minutes after I'm done cleaning up Lightning."[i]

I headed over to the house and Kathy had a plate set out for me at the table. We had breakfast with the whole family, and then Tim, Christa, and I piled into her car, and we were on our way to church.

"Okay, Christa, help me understand," I said. "You drive. You own a car. You have a smartphone. But you live on an Amish farm. How does this all work?" I'd had enough of circling the wagon on these questions. I needed some clarity.

---

i. I assumed Lightning was the horse and not the buggy. Although, how kick butt would it be to have a buggy named Lightning?

Christa explained that she decided to leave the Amish church a few years ago. And Tim left last year and was baptized into the Mennonite Church. They just decided that the Amish way wasn't going to be their way moving forward.

"Mom and Dad were really good about it," Christa said. "Ya know, I'm sure they wish we'd stayed Amish, but they still love us and support us. They are great parents. And although I'm no longer Amish, I still get so many of the benefits of living among them. I grew up Amish and wouldn't change my childhood for anything. I'm still just as intertwined with the relationships I had before I left the church. Everyone has been so supportive. We are all just trying to figure the world out one day at a time."

What?! This is *not* how the Amish had been portrayed on the shows I'd watched on TV. I know there are different orders of Amish. And as the orders get more and more conservative, the rules get stricter. Was I at a super liberal, progressive Amish order? I had *soo* many questions.

Church was amazing. And guess what happened after church? That's right. They moved all the chairs out, set up tables, and we had a gigantic meal together. *The meals.* And not only was the food amazing, something else was amazing too. Although the Mennonites are allowed to have phones—and I'm assuming that most of the people there had phones—nobody had them out. Everyone was just laughing and talking and eating. No phones in sight. These humans had smartphones in their pockets and purses and never pulled them out. Not to take a photo, not to check a message, not to scroll Instagram. They were in charge of their phones; their phones were not in charge of them.

I was sitting at a newly set up table with Christa and Tim after going through the buffet line when a shocked-sounding voice boomed from behind me. "OMG, Loswhit? Why are you here? I follow you on Instagram! Why are you at my little church?"

Crazy. Y'all are everywhere.

When we got home from church that afternoon, Willis was about to bike into town to pick up a part for his tractor.

"I got it! I can do it!" I insisted.

"Are you sure? You're going to have to pull a little mini trailer or wagon behind the bike," he said.

"No problem. I got it. I wanna do something Amish by myself," I proudly decreed.

Willis chuckled. "Riding a bike isn't only Amish, you know." Willis got jokes.

I strapped a bike helmet on my shiny bald head and asked Willis to give me directions.

"Okay, you're going to turn right out of the driveway," he began. "And the highway is pretty busy right now, so if I were you, I would take the first right that you come to. That is gonna take you about a mile and a half down a country road. Watch for manure. Then you will come to a four-way stop. You are going to turn left there and then make your first right. That will take you to Highway 43. Turn right on 43, and the tractor store will be about one mile down on the right."

I stared at him blankly. *Does he expect me to remember all of that?* He was looking at me as if he did. "Can you repeat that one more time?" I asked. So he did. This time, he made more emphatic hand motions. He never once thought to walk inside and grab a piece of paper to write down the directions. No. He just assumed I could actually remember. *Lord, have mercy.*

I started mumbling the directions over and over to myself to make sure I wouldn't forget. I got on the bike and slowly made my way down the gravel driveway.

"Please be careful, Carlos!" Kathy called out from where she was hanging sheets on the laundry line to dry.

I took a right and knew the next thing I needed to do was turn right again. So far so good. I had a slick-looking helmet and was also wearing a bright yellow traffic-reflector vest. I was looking impressive, if I do say so myself. I pedaled another few hundred yards, keeping a tight grip on the handlebars because cars were *flying* past me. *"Slow down, man!"* I yelled as a semi literally went by so fast it made my bike swerve in the wind.

I pedaled hard and fast until I came to a street and took a right. I was only fifty feet onto the street when I felt like I could relax. No more cars flying by. No more semis. And the farm I was riding by was gorgeous. Manicured lawn. Flowers dancing in the wind as if God himself had planted them there earlier this morning.

Everything was perfect, so I did that thing you do when you feel free and content on a bike. You know, when you let go of the handlebars and sway left and right. I felt like I was back in 1985, cruising through my old childhood neighborhood in Decatur, Georgia. I couldn't remember the last time I had ridden a bike like this. Well, the truth is, I had never ridden a bike like this because there is one detail I haven't let you in on yet. The bike was electric. That's right, an e-bike. The Amish are *flying around* Holmes County, Ohio, on e-bikes. In fact, you see more e-bikes on the roads than you do horses and buggies.

The Millers had two really fast e-bikes that they charged with the generator they have on their farm. I know, I know, that's confusing, right? But I'll clear it up for you later. For now, just know that I was not pedaling at all. No effort was being expended by yours truly. I was just gliding through these backcountry roads taking in all the beautiful scenery they had to offer.

About five minutes into my blissful glide, I had my first oh-crap moment. I had taken a few turns since turning off the main highway. *Where am I? Is this road supposed to dead end? Am I supposed to go left or right? Did I miss my turn?* I tried to recall Willis's directions, but they were completely gone. I remembered nothing but the last direction—that the tractor store would be a mile down the road on the right. But I didn't know what road that was. Nor did I know the name of the tractor store. I assumed there was only one of those in such a small town. But I didn't know if this tractor store was even in this town. *Ugh.* I was 100 percent officially lost.

I didn't have a phone.

I didn't have directions.

I had only this e-bike. I tried to backtrack, but nothing looked the same going the other direction. Before I knew it, I had taken a few turns that I quickly learned were not the correct turns. I was headed down a really steep road I hadn't ridden up. So when I got to the bottom I just stopped. I got off my bike and tried to collect my thoughts and figure this out.

"Okay, Carlos. Just relax. You have been lost before. You can find your way back," I said aloud. But the truth is, I couldn't remember the last time I'd been this lost.

When have we ever been lost since we've had smartphones? We actually almost *can't* get lost anymore. It's impossible. We always have our phones with us. And unless they die or we lose service in the middle of a trip, we won't be lost. Which means getting lost is yet another thing we have lost the ability to do.

I was panicked because I didn't know what to do. *What if nobody comes by or offers to help? Should I just keep going? Am I getting farther away or getting closer?*

We don't get lost anymore. We trust our little GPS maps with our lives. We don't even think twice when the voice on our map app tells us to go left or right or turn in nine hundred feet.[ii]

Is using a GPS bad for us? Should we get lost more? On the face of it, of course GPS is good. We get lost less and are more efficient with our time. I mean, our apps will even reroute us around traffic. It's really a valuable tool. But guess what? I realized that after what I thought was about a forty-minute bike ride—it felt like forty minutes but I didn't have a phone or a watch, so how was I supposed to know—I couldn't remember a single thing Willis had told me. I'd lost the ability to remember directions.

That's a consequence of our reliance on GPS—that we have lost our internal GPS skills. John Silcox, a London photographer and writer whose work takes him around the globe, cites a study that suggests getting lost and using our internal GPS to navigate our way out is actually good for us. He wrote:

> A 2006 study scanning the brains of London taxi drivers found that the hippocampi, the regions responsible for direction, increased in volume and developed neuron-dense grey matter as the drivers memorized the layout of the city. Individuals who frequently navigate complex environments the old-fashioned way, by identifying landmarks, literally grow their brains. Additionally, many studies show that having a smaller, weaker hippocampus makes you more vulnerable to brain diseases such as Alzheimer's, since it's one of the first regions affected.[1]

---

ii. Dear Siri, I do not know now, nor will I ever know, how far nine hundred feet is. Anyways.

After a few minutes of panic, I began to hear the now-familiar sound of horse hooves clopping along the street. I turned around and saw a horse and buggy fast approaching. Okay, maybe not so fast. But approaching. I waved them down, and inside the buggy was a young man, maybe thirteen, and an older woman, maybe in her seventies.

"Hey, there!" I said. "So sorry to bother you. Thanks for stopping. I think I'm lost. Could you—"

The young man interrupted me. "You the man that's living with the Miller family for a bit?" he asked.

"Oh, yeah, that's me. How'd you know?" The second those words came flying out of my mouth I felt like an idiot. What other bald, Black, tattooed man is riding around this part of the planet? Just me.

"Where you looking to go?" he asked.

After a few seconds, he knew exactly where I was going, and he had me follow him a mile back the other direction until we came to a stop sign. "This is as far as I can guide you, but you are only about fifteen minutes away now. Just head down this road and when you hit the four-way stop, turn left. That's the only turn you gotta remember. You will run right into it."

"Thanks, kid!" I yelled, and I pedaled away.

When I hit the four-way stop, there was a woman there retrieving her mail. When I greeted her, she said, "You the one at the Miller farm?"

I've never felt more like a local celebrity. "Why, yes! That's me! I'm Carlos," I said.

"Hi, Carlos," she said. "I hear you are coming to our church service on Sunday. Buckle up! That should be fun!"

Wait, what? Nobody told me this. Her kids were in the yard playing, and I asked if I could kick the ball with them. She obliged. There I was. A man completely out of his comfort zone, or zone in general, playing kickball with a few cute Amish kids in their front yard. We played for a few minutes before I was on my way again.

When I finally reached my destination and walked into the tractor store, the guy at the counter said, "You must be Willis's friend." Again. Famous.

"The part is back on the driveway. Follow me," he said. "Took you a little longer to get here than I thought. Willis let me know you were coming. Did you get lost?"

Did I get lost?

"Well, getting lost is good for ya," he said. "We are getting dumber, ya know. Getting lost makes you smarter."

I had been gone an hour already, and the entire trip was supposed to take twenty minutes. Going back was faster as I just stayed on the kamikaze highway. Lord, have mercy, these non-Amish needed *to slow down*! I made it home in fifteen minutes.

I got lost. And I ended up making three new friends because of it! I also had to figure things out that I don't normally have to figure out. There was something invigorating about it.

So I guess the point of this story is to encourage you to get lost too. Seriously! Do it. We rely *way* too much on these phones to get us from point A to point B. What if you tried to get lost at least once a week?

Perhaps you're shaking your head and thinking, "No way." If so, I understand. I know the idea of getting lost may be terrifying for some. Why? Well, because many of us have memories of getting lost that predate our cell phones. One of my most traumatic childhood memories is losing my mom in a mall. I had to sit with a smelly mall security officer for what felt like days until my mom tracked me down.

But listen, I'm not saying throw the phone away. Just turn off the navigation every now and then. You can still call for help if you end up more lost than you want to be. Plus, there are some legit benefits you may not experience any other way. Let's list some out—why it's important for you to get lost sometimes.

1. **YOU WILL DISCOVER NEW PLACES**. Literally. The number of times I got lost over my two weeks in Ohio are too many to count. And every single time, I met someone new or found something new. Just imagine how much bigger your world can get when you discover your new favorite coffee shop because you spent a few extra minutes wandering around a neighborhood instead of making a beeline to your destination using the "fastest route" and "avoid tolls" settings on Google Maps. What if by getting lost on the way to work or exploring the side streets you run across a beautiful view or an under-the-radar park? You'll never know unless you get lost!

2. **YOU WILL KEEP YOUR BRAIN FRESH**. The guy at the tractor store was right—getting lost is good for ya. When we rely only on things humans have never relied on before (smartphones), and when we don't have to think about things the way we used to, we allow parts of our brain that once were strong to atrophy. As a man who has a father with dementia, keeping my brain strong and firing all the time is important!

3. **YOU WILL FIND THAT NOT HAVING A VOICE BARKING DIRECTIONS AT EVERY TURN IS REFRESHING**. You don't know how much you hear Siri directing every single moment of your life until she is no longer talking. Tell her to get lost! Also know that your phone won't work everywhere in the world, which means you need to be able to figure out

directions without your phone. I make my kids do this all the time. They have to get from point A to B without using their phones. It's worth it!

Friend, I'm telling you, getting lost has become one of my new favorite hobbies. I now leave my phone in my hotel room sometimes as I venture through a new city looking for a bite to eat or coffee to drink. And you know what's even more freeing? Not using Yelp and not trusting someone else's taste buds with my own. I mean, what a horrible idea Yelp has turned out to be. We are missing out on so many amazing restaurants because we are letting someone else rate them instead of us.

Anyway, it's time, friend.

I've always wanted to say this to somebody . . . *Get lost!*

CHAPTER 17

COMMUNITY

"This Thursday is my dad's birthday," Willis said as we were strapping up the horses in the barn. "Now, you don't have to if you don't want to, but all my siblings and their spouses are going to take Doddy to his favorite restaurant. And it's gonna be a surprise. You are more than welcome to come. I think you will really enjoy the food."

We were getting the horses ready for a day of tedding the hay. That's right. Tedding the hay. That basically meant we were going to run a machine called a tedder behind the horses to scatter out the grass so it could dry before we raked and baled it. But beyond being impressed by my incredible knowledge of making hay—that I'm certain is blowing you away right now—I want you to be impressed with something else. I need you to be impressed that I am now so much a part of the Miller family's life *that I am going to a birthday dinner for Doddy.* I mean, go ahead and give me my Amish card. I'm in.

"I would be honored," I said. "Where are we going?"

Now, listen. I had already eaten at a few hole-in-the-wall, or hole-in-the-pasture, kind of spots in the eight days I'd been there, and all of them were incredible. I couldn't wait to head to Doddy's favorite Amish hole-in-the-wall.

"Oh, you may have heard of it," Willis said. "It is actually incredible. Their T-bone steak is amazing. And the carrot cake is even better!" This sounded like my kind of Amish spot. I was beginning to salivate.

"Is it here in Mount Hope or another small town?" I asked.

"Oh, no. It's much nicer than anywhere around here. We are heading to Canton. My brother is renting a fifteen-passenger van, and we are all going to ride together. The place is called Golden Corral. And if you have never been, it's really, really good."

Did Willis just hype up Golden Corral? Like, did that just happen? Did he just talk about their T-bone steak as if it were from a five-star steak house? Why, yes. Yes, he did. But if a man loved himself some Golden Corral, then who was I to complain?

Although Doddy lived on the farm, I didn't see him much, except for at dinner. He spent some of his time volunteering at the thrift store two towns over. He also spent a lot of time reading and listening to music in his recliner. Although he lived in a smaller house only a few feet away from the main farmhouse, he never missed dinner with the rest of the family. He was just as much a part of the community as anyone else, and I loved how there was never a second thought about including him in everything. He was not an afterthought. He was still all-in. I'm certain that had to feel good for him. As I watch my parents age, I know how loneliness can creep in.

I started to realize that there was much more beneath the surface and beneath what I had always assumed about Amish people. Like, I'd already learned that they didn't kick their kids out if they decided that the Amish way wasn't for them, and I discovered that they have different ways they can power their homes since no Amish are on public utilities. Some power them by battery but most by generator. I realized that they don't just travel by horse and buggy but also ride e-bikes. *What?* There was something I was missing though. *If they can do all this stuff, then why don't they just go all-in? There is so much more they could experience out there if they just leveled up their technology a bit more.*

"Willis, I need you to help me," I said. "Instead of me asking you every single time something else about the Amish confuses me, may I just ask you one question? I think this may be the question that answers them all. What is the deal with you and technology? Like, why some technologies and not others? Who decides? Why are we taking a freaking fifteen-passenger van to Golden Corral in Canton? Is that because the horse and buggy would just take too long? What gives?"

Willis didn't skip a beat.

"Community, Carlos," he said. "The community is more important than anything else. Community is more important than individuality. Community is more important than technology. So we just want to make sure that anything we do enriches the community. It's not that we don't believe in cars or that cars are evil. That's not it at all. We just know that if we started using cars, then our community would no longer be, well, a community."

It was starting to make sense. "Say more," I said.

"Think about it," he said. "Who lives four houses down from you in Nashville?"

"Um, I'm embarrassed to say this, but I don't know."

"Well, there is the first problem," he chuckled. "Do you know any of your neighbors?"

"Of course I do!" And I started rattling them off with a bit more smugness than appropriate—because after I said five names, I was stumped. *Man, I really needed to meet people in my neighborhood. This is embarrassing.*

"Okay, you mentioned Grey," Willis said. "He's your older next-door neighbor, right? What would happen if his house burned down tonight?"

He isn't giving me much to go on. Is this a trick question?

"Um, I hope someone would call 911, right?"

"Yes, but after his house burns down. What would you do?"

"Well, I would probably call to make sure he was okay and then ask what he needs." *Where is Willis going with this?*

"How would you get home?" he asked.

"Well, I guess I would fly home," I replied.

"You see, Carlos, here is how we are living different in our community than you do in yours. Our community is an actual community." I don't think he knew just how bad he was burning me right then, so I gave him the benefit of the doubt and let him keep going.

"If we all had cars, and we were spread all over Ohio doing different things tonight, and if Mrs. Yoder's house burned down, we would never have been able to rebuild her home in four days flat—which we did. If we had cars, we couldn't have done that because we would be too far apart from each other. So we like to keep it close. It's not that cars are evil; it's that if we allowed cars into our communities, we would lose the very fabric of what our communities are all about. And that is just cars. It goes on and on."

He didn't even have to continue. I was already getting it. Like, I seriously felt as if I'd been hit by an Amish left hook. It made me think about when I used to drive forty minutes to this church I used to work at. It was an amazing church. But I was driving forty minutes. I was not going to church in my actual community. Now, not everyone needs to go to a church around the corner from their house. But it just made me wonder if we were doing life way more spread apart than we were created to.

Willis continued. "Every choice we make about our communities is always to make sure that the community thrives and grows closer. Not farther apart. There are some pieces of technology that we allow because they aren't going to grow us apart. For example, e-bikes. They can go about as far as a horse and buggy with a single charge. And they are less work than a horse. Now, some of our churches don't allow e-bikes but they do allow electric scooters. We call this group the Danners or the Dan Church. They are a really conservative subgroup of Old Order Amish. You will see them scooting around. Their church deacons made a decision that e-bikes would be too easy to get around on, so scooters it is. We differ in that. But what you won't ever see in an Amish community is a TV. That's something that will never get in. Why? Well, I'm certain I don't have to tell you why. I'm sure you see it yourself."

Why did Willis feel the need to attack my soul like this? He was absolutely right. I'm fairly certain I could have been a billionaire had I not spent so many years of my life in front of that thing. Okay, maybe not a billionaire. But I would have definitely lived a lot more life. Not to mention the amount of stuff we now have to shield our kids' eyes from (and our own!).

"So community is the number one thing we think about when we consider whether to allow in a certain piece of technology," Willis continued. "And it normally takes a *long* time to get in. Because once you give something, it's much harder to take it away. And, of course, we always want to honor God with everything we do. Even how we live in community."

While Willis was explaining all of this to me, I could feel my spirit *longing* for the kind of community he described. I'm not ready to become Amish. But man, to not have to worry if something would be taken care of? That's next level. Like Doddy—he doesn't want for anything. His community is taking care of him.

"How about health care? Do you guys have health care?" I asked.

"Oh, we don't have to worry about any of that. If someone is sick, we all pitch in to cover the bills. Nobody has to worry about it. And if we don't have enough money, we will have a community auction, and people will donate some of their personal belongings to auction off so that the person in need is taken care of."

What in the actual freaking world?

It got me thinking. What does my community *actually* look like? I am a part of an incredible church. Like, mind-blowingly incredible. But I can tell you something, I barely know anyone. The church is gigantic. And you would think that bigger is better. But not when you think about community like the Amish do. And to be fair, there are non-Amish churches that have great communities, and they make them smaller by doing Sunday school and small groups and the like. Even so, it's not the same. Not at all.

There is not a single person who is a part of the Amish community who has to worry whether something they need will be taken care of. I'm serious. Every real need is taken care of by the community.

My conversation with Willis got me thinking about the way many of us do community now. I talk to a lot of very connected people— people who, from a distance, look like they have more friends than they know what to do with. But most of them tell me they are actually lonely and wish they had more friends. We are the most digitally connected generation in the history of planet Earth and it would not be a stretch to say that we are also the loneliest.

Watching groups of friends choose to stare at their phones rather than engaging with each other when they are together is, if you think about it, insane. If you had beamed into our current reality from 1980 and saw friends doing that, you would think they were avoiding each other because they didn't want to be together. This is a problem.

The Amish will never have this problem because they won't allow themselves to. They aren't anti-technology; they are pro-community. So they weigh the potential value of every piece of new technology before allowing it.

We don't have to give up technology to have community, but we *can* be more intentional about the limits we place on technology that may be hindering us in finding true community. If you don't have a thriving community where you live, I have good news—you *can* find one. If you do have a thriving community, I have good news for you too—you can make it better.

1. **START VISITING**. The Amish *love* to visit. In fact, visiting is almost as important as eating. To be fair, they never eat alone. They are always visiting over meals. I now make it a point to schedule a few "visits" with friends each week. I've even weirded out my friends by asking them if we can have a visit. They don't know what to do. But I love it. Let's text less and visit more.

2. **ASK YOURSELF IF THE NEXT PIECE OF TECHNOLOGY IS GOING TO ENHANCE OR DIMINISH YOUR COMMUNITY.** The answer may surprise you because technology isn't always something to remove. The Amish make use of some technology for the purpose of *enhancing* community. I mean, we rode in a fifteen-passenger van—a gigantic piece of technology— because it allowed us to have community and do it on the way

177

to having a juicy T-bone steak at Golden Corral! But seriously, ask yourself what technology you can cut out and what can be brought in to enhance your sense of community. When we bought our PlayStation5, it quickly became a hub for my kids' friends. They all come over and play. I count that as a technology win.

3. **MOVE YOUR COMMUNITY OFFLINE**. If there is anyone who knows how important and impactful online community is, it's me. I've watched the Instafamilia literally change people's lives for the better. Online community is good. But it will *never* replace face-to-face relationships. I've made some great friends online, but nothing was better than meeting those same people offline. Again, hear me say that if some of your community is online, that is fine. I would just push you to try to increase your face-to-face community over your thumb-to-thumb community.

The Amish don't do community perfectly. But they *do* do it intentionally. That is what I am taking away from my time with them. I desired so much of what they had because it was something that could always be counted on. And if there is something we are all missing and searching for these days, it's something to rely on. Can you imagine living in that kind of deep, intentional, true community? Knowing that your neighbors will be there for you, no matter what?

I guess I better go meet my neighbors. How embarrassing.

CHAPTER 18

INTUITION

Making hay is more complicated than I ever imagined it to be. I've seen hay bales rolled up along every highway in America, and it never occurred to me that it involved anything more than cutting the hay and rolling the hay.

After seven days on this farm, I realized that almost every decision we made was about the hay. Should we cut the field of grass to make fresh hay? Should we rake the already-cut grass to roll the hay? Should we tedder the field again to dry the hay out some more? Is it going to rain tomorrow? Because if it is, we can't cut the hay; but if it doesn't rain, then we should cut the hay and roll the other fields of hay.

Remember, if you get any of this wrong, you ruin an entire field of hay. And if you have only a few fields, that could be seven to eight months of growing that can go bad in a matter of days. And if your hay goes bad, then what are the horses and sheep going to eat in the winter? Because if you don't have hay, you have to then buy it, which then forces you to spend money you don't have, and then within a year your farm goes bust.

I was starting to get more stressed out about the hay situation than Willis was.

This making-hay business was a lot to process, and I couldn't get over the fact that Willis was relying on his gut for most of his decision-making. Like, he wasn't on Google all day and didn't have all these hay cutting apps, which I'm sure exist, to tell him when the best time to cut the hay was going to be.

To be fair, Willis did have a flip phone. And he was always calling his friends and family, who are also farmers, to ask what they thought about the weather and the forecast. And every year that pool of farmers got smaller and smaller because it was getting harder and harder for them to keep their heads above water.

Now, everything I said in the last chapter about the community making sure everyone's taken care of is true. And I'm sure that if one farm had a disastrous mishap with the hay, the community would be there to support them. But that doesn't mean there aren't real challenges and vulnerabilities, even for a tight-knit community like the Amish. Farming is hard work with few guarantees—and lots of things that can go wrong.

"Most of the Amish have given up farming for other trades," Willis told me one night as we sat on the patio drinking coffee. "And it kind of makes me sad. You see, the Amish, we are farmers. That is where our roots are. But it's become harder and harder to make farms profitable. All my growing up, this farm was a dairy farm. My daddy woke up before the sun to milk all those cows. And even with the introduction of mechanical milking tools, we just couldn't keep up. So I had to switch the entire farm from a dairy farm to a sheep farm a few years ago."

"So you're saying you didn't grow up farming sheep?" I asked. That was crazy to me.

"No. I've only been farming sheep for about four years," he said.

"Well, who taught you?" I asked.

"Oh, I went to sheep school," he said. "It was about two weeks long, and I learned everything I needed to learn. And then I made a lot of mistakes along the way. Now I think I'm getting the hang of it."

I need both of us to sit back for a moment and consider whether we could buy one hundred sheep, go to a sheep school for two weeks, and then go do it. *Hahahahaha!* I mean, I'm laughing at the thought. I'd only been there seven days and I had learned more than I ever wanted to learn about sheep, but I still couldn't figure out how to get them to listen to a dang thing I said. I did know that in a few days Willis was going to teach me to shear a sheep, and I was half terrified and half pumped to be able to add a new life skill to my tool belt.

"You just have to believe in yourself," Willis said. "Trust your gut. I knew it was in me."

Every single morning, as I was on my way to the farmhouse for breakfast, I saw Doddy standing in the middle of the field behind his house. Some mornings he stood there and simply looked off into the distance. Other days I'd see him bend over and pick some grass. So I asked Willis one morning what his dad was up to.

"This is the first year Doddy can't drive the horses," Willis said. "So I reckon he is just out there to be one with the earth that he farmed for so many years. He definitely misses it. But the horses are just too much for him now. He will go out there every day and report back to me. I trust him more than I trust anyone when it comes to this land. *He* knows it."

Just then, I heard Doddy walk up behind us and say something, but not in English. Some Amish communities speak what's called Pennsylvania Dutch, which is actually a German dialect.

"He said the hay needs one more day of drying before we roll it," Willis said. And then Doddy turned around and walked back to his house.

"So tomorrow we roll this hay and then cut the other field?" I asked, sounding and feeling more like a farmer than I ever have in my entire life.[i]

"Yippers," Will replied. That meant yes.

"Okay! It's the day I've been waiting for since I got here!" I said. And it was. I had learned a lot about the sheep. I'd been out in the pasture with the sheep day after day. I had seen Willis and his sheep dog herd the sheep into pens and helped corral them. But I was ready to take on a new challenge. I couldn't wait to get behind those gigantic Anheuser Busch–looking horses with my Amish hat and yell, *"Gee!"* and *"Haw!"* to direct them left and right. I felt like that was going to be a rite of passage. And Willis told me I was going to be able to do it on my own, without him.

Let's go!

I went to bed that night with all the butterflies of a five-year-old kid on Christmas morning. I was *pumped.*

I woke up around 4:00 a.m. to the loudest thunderclap right outside my door. I sat straight up in bed only to have my forehead hit the ceiling. I forgot I was asleep in a loft.

"OMG, I'm bleeding!" I said. So I stumbled down the obstacle course of the loft and the ladder to the bathroom to see the crack in my head and the blood that was most certainly about to drip down my face. But when I turned on the light and looked in the mirror, I saw no cut and no blood. *Why am I the way I am?*

I crawled back in bed feeling a bit dejected because I was *really*

---

i. Like, I know my wife thinks I'm attractive, but I honestly don't know if she would be able to keep her hands off me if I started talking about hay and the weather and when it should be cut or raked. I pray five times a day and talk about farming? I'm an Amish monk.

looking forward to cutting the hay today. But, alas, a storm had rolled in. I guess we were going to have to wait at least four more days for the hay and grass to dry. Bummed, I closed my eyes and went back to sleep for a few more hours. No need for a sound machine because I had one right outside my window. The thunder was relentless.

Six a.m. came quickly, and I got up and made my way to the farmhouse. Dark clouds were thick overhead, but it didn't look like it had rained on the farm. I was sure it would any minute. The sky was nearly black. I started running toward the farmhouse so I wouldn't get caught in the storm.

"What's the plan, WilLos?" I asked Willis as we were eating breakfast. That's right. Me and my new Amish BFF have a nickname. When we are together, I call us WilLos. Willis + Carlos = WilLos. Cute, I know.

"Well, the plan is the same," Willis said. "You and Kathy are gonna go visit Diane and Ed, and Ed is gonna show you around the horse farm. Then you will come back after lunch, and we will head out to the north field and start cutting the hay. Big day!" (Remember, Diane is Willis and Kathy's oldest daughter.)

Now, listen. I know I had been a sheep farmer for only a few days, but I straight up interjected the obvious. "Um, Willis, have you looked outside? You see those clouds a few hundred yards away? You hear the thunder? That is rain. Like, the wet kind. I thought you said that wet hay goes bad, so we have to wait to cut and bale it."

Willis had such a cute smirk on his face. And I say cute with all the respect a hardworking Amish farmer deserves. "It's not gonna rain, Carlos," Willis said with the same degree of confidence I'd had when telling him it was for sure going to rain.

"What do you mean, man?" I said. "Look outside. That's rain. And it's heading this direction."

"Come out here," Willis said as he got up from the table. "Walk with me out into the field."

I followed him, thunder rattling not too far away.

When we were standing in the middle of the field, he said, "Look at your boots." I looked down. "You see they are wet, that there's dew on your boots? My daddy used to always say, 'If there's dew on your boots, it's not gonna rain.'"

Okay, I'd heard enough of this nonsense. "I'm sure that may be true sometimes, but *look up*. There's dew on my boots *and* it's raining." I swear I felt a raindrop hit my head.

"It's not gonna rain. I feel it in my gut, and I see it on my boots."

I was convinced this man was going to ruin seven months of waiting for this harvest, and I was going to have to experience the devastation of it on the front row. I was not looking forward to the afternoon.

"I'm gonna go ahead and start cutting," Willis said, "and then when you get back this afternoon, you can help rake. How's that sound?"

"It sounds like a bad idea," I said. "But it's your grass, man." I loved that I was confident enough with Willis that I was now *judging* his farming. Who had I become?

We got into Christa's car and headed toward Diane and Ed's farm. It was about ten miles away. We decided on the car instead of the horse and buggy because—wait for it—it was probably going to rain.

I had an incredible morning at the horse farm. Ed showed me the racehorses he trains for a living. Ed's son, Willis's grandson, was running in and out of the barn, in between the horses' legs, and jumping from ten-foot ladders. He was breaking every rule I ever had for my suburban kids in a matter of ten minutes.

After lunch Christa, Kathy, and I hopped back into the car and headed home. When I tell you that three minutes after we left Ed and Diane's it started to rain, I mean that it started to *dump*. And the second the heavens opened, I could feel the tension in the car. We were only about five miles from the farm and things weren't looking good. About two minutes from the farm, we hit the four-way stop in Mount Hope. The look of concern on Kathy's face was unmistakable. As in, I could feel her pain. All that time growing. All that time figuring out if the alfalfa was ready to cut. All the sheep they were going to have to buy hay for. Christa looked at me through the rearview mirror with an expression that said, *Oh, crap.*

The empathetic part of me couldn't hold it in. "I'm so sorry, Kathy. This sucks. Maybe it will dry out over the next few days, and it won't all go to waste." I tried to offer some compassion to a farmer's wife, but I wasn't very good at it.

"Willis said there was dew on his boots," Kathy said. "So it's not gonna rain." Her gaze was fixed straight ahead on County Road 45, straight toward their farm. It was still dumping rain when we pulled through the intersection. To let you know how close to the farm we were at that point, it takes me five minutes on the e-bike to get from the driveway of the farm to town. So we were about ninety seconds away by car.

What I'm about to tell you would feel like the biggest fabrication and exaggeration of a story if I hadn't had two Amish witnesses sitting with me at the time of this miracle. Well, one Amish woman and one Mennonite woman, both filled with honor and conviction.

When we were about half a mile from the farm, my jaw dropped. The road went from soaking wet to dry. Not like it slowly stopped raining, and not like it had rained here and the cloud had moved past and left everything wet. No. It was like we hit a line of rain that was running parallel to their farm. Everything was completely dry.

All the muscles in Kathy's face relaxed. I was blown away. When we turned onto the driveway, Willis was standing in the road by the barn, arms crossed, next to his four horses, fresh from a few hours of cutting hay.

I got out of the car and we both started laughing, almost uncontrollably. I just shook my head and stared him right in the eyes.

"There was dew on my boots," he said.

———

You know what we don't *dew* anymore? Sorry, I had to. I'll retype that for my editor. You know what we don't *do* anymore? We don't trust our gut. And why would we? I already talked about how we rely so much on GPS that we don't get lost anymore. But it's not just GPS. It's so much more.

In today's world we have come to rely on external sources for every decision we make.

Going to dinner? Yelp.

Going fishing? Fish-finder app.

Want to watch a movie on Netflix? Just go to the most recommended section.

We have access to so much data from other people or AI that we don't even have to process our own decisions like we used to. And don't get me started on restaurant and coffee-shop reviews. Because it's a fifty-fifty shot if the reviews are legit. And if we have only a 50 percent shot of it sucking or not sucking, why in the world would we allow the taste buds of complete strangers to be the drivers of our decision-making?

We have lost our gut-checking skills, our instinct. Our overreliance on external data has legitimately crushed our trust in our own intuition. Why rely on it when you have the hard data of 345 three-star reviewers on Google?

You do realize that you have the capacity to make basic life decisions without external input from people you don't know, right? Intuition is built on your accumulated experience, and it is vital for navigating life, helping you make quick decisions, and even for connecting with people you might not otherwise have ever connected with. So let your intuition do its work.

Here are three things I've put into place so I can begin to wake up my intuition after years of slumber.

1. **NO MORE REVIEWS.** If it's a hole in the wall, chances are you have a Spidey sense of whether it's going to keep you in the bathroom all night or if you'll be eating there repeatedly and bringing all your friends. The number of people who told me Whataburger was better than In-N-Out was overwhelming, but every single time I have ever driven by a Whataburger it has been empty; every single time I have driven by an In-N-Out, there has been a line wrapped around the block. Enter *gut* check. I still love you, Whataburger fans. Just know that I don't trust anything you say anymore. Trust. Your. Gut.

2. **WRITE DOWN DIRECTIONS BEFORE LEAVING.** Use a napkin or the back of a CVS receipt. Remember MapQuest? Go buy yourself a printer and print out directions like it's 2004 again. That's a happy medium between the possibility of getting lost and having to trust your God-given intuition.

3. **PRAY ABOUT THE LITTLE THINGS IN LIFE, NOT JUST THE BIG THINGS.** It seems like the only time we pray for guidance is when we can't find the answers we need on our smartphones. And I get it. Why pray about things if we can get what we need from a Google search? Why would God care about our lunch choices? To which I might respond, why *wouldn't* God care? What have you got to lose by praying

about where to have coffee tomorrow? Add God to the Yelp convos and watch some incredible things begin to happen in your day-to-day.

———

So don't even think that I don't regularly try to predict the weather by walking into my front yard in the morning to see if there is dew on my boots—or my Nike Air Max. Because I do. And you know what, most of the time, *it works*!

Trust your gut. God's in it.

CHAPTER 19

UNOFFENDED

Remember how much swagger I had at the thought of driving horses and plowing the fields? Well, that lasted about ninety seconds after I started driving Willis's giant, horse-drawn hay rake. I was supposed to be taking the horses from north to south in neat rows, but before long it ended up looking like I was in a game of tag. The horses and I were being chased by Willis, and we weren't about to get caught.

Here's the funny part. Not only was Willis chasing after me and his four horses, he had my GoPro in his hand while chasing us. Oh, to have been a tourist driving the pristine and beautiful backroads of Holmes County, Ohio, Amish Country, and seeing an Amish man running through his field as fast as he can holding a GoPro in one hand and his hat in the other while a Black man in an Amish hat steers four horses pulling a hay rake in a zigzag. This is the stuff reality shows are made of. Lucky for you, the GoPro captured most of it, so I'm certain I'll be able to post a clip in which you'll get to hear Willis cursing in Pennsylvania Dutch.

I wasn't aware of how badly this was going until Willis finally caught up to me and said, "I think one of the horses got a little spooked. Could have come across a fox hole or something." Spooked? What was he talking about? From my perspective, I had crushed my first solo four-horse drive. Until I looked behind me. Receipts don't lie. And the receipt that I had turned in was about one hundred yards long and looked the shape of a strand of crimped hair from 1995.

I gave back the reins to Willis and sat beside him. We continued back and forth across the field. Finishing the job we had started together. It felt good. I felt like I belonged.

My farming lessons were going as well as you might imagine. I'm a quick learner, and I began to feel a little bummed that by the time I really started to get the hang of a few of the things around the farm, it would be time to go. But every time I began to wallow in my sadness that this whole thing was coming to an end, there was another adventure around the corner. And the next few hours were no different.

About day ten I was feeling pretty much as Amish as I probably ever would and had a swagger about me. I was riding that e-bike all over the county and getting waved at by every horse and buggy I passed along the way. I'd met new people every day and had been in all the local businesses. I felt like part of the community. But the one thing I hadn't done yet was go to one of their regular livestock auctions and flea markets. The Mount Hope Auction was coming up, and it would be held right there in town, just on the other side of the four-way stop. It's a huge operation. Animals everywhere. Amish people everywhere. And then there was me. I was everywhere too.

When Willis went to auction off some of his lambs, I decided to walk around from one auction to another. At one point I had to use the restroom and there was a long line. You know what the craziest part of that moment was? Not one single man in line was looking at a phone. Men were making small talk as they stood in line. Same thing happened in the lunch line. Everybody was chatting. Looking each other in the eye. I mean, both of those situations are definite *no eye contact* in my world. But here it was different. They had never gotten to the point in their day-to-day lives where they stopped looking each other in the eye.

And I actually got sad. Because this is how it's supposed to be. It's not supposed to be the way we do it. Since my experiment ended I've tried my hardest to look people in the eye everywhere I go, but the amount of stranger-danger stares I get back is sad. When I smiled at a lady at the grocery store the other day, she looked at me suspiciously and said, "What are you looking at?" Like she was almost offended I was looking at her and smiling. It's all wrong in our world when it comes to this. It made me want to run back to the bathroom line at the Mount Hope Auction.

So back to the auction we will go.

I had to keep reminding myself that I wasn't Amish. Also, that I didn't want to be Amish. When you are submerged into a subculture, and you are leaving said subculture within a few days, you tend to look at it through rose-colored glasses. And every once in a while, those glasses fall off.

I was getting ready to leave the auction, so I swung by Kathy's office to say goodbye before taking my e-bike back to the farm. Kathy works at the auction, and she'd introduced me to her coworker, who said, "So you're a monk?" Kathy laughed and I said, "Yes. Yes, I'm a monk."

I walked out the door and found my e-bike. I picked my yellow reflector vest out of the basket I carried all my stuff in and grabbed my helmet. This was one of two fancy Bluetooth helmets Kathy and Willis use so they can talk to each other while riding around together. *Look at the Amish!* Willis was basically the Amish Steve Jobs.

As I was strapping on my helmet I started to feel something I had not felt in a long time—I started to feel eyeballs all around me. See, my bike was surrounded by at least sixty other e-bikes. All parked right next to each other. Nobody had bike locks on their bikes. And when I looked up, I saw about five Amish men staring a hole through me. And I was so accustomed to being Amish at that point that I didn't even get it. When I started backing the bike out of the bike rack, a few more Amish men started looking at me. Actually, they were beginning to walk toward me. Then it hit me. *Carlos, you are a Black, bald man with tattoos getting on an e-bike that only Amish own. Of course they think you are about to steal it.*

I had to make a quick decision. *Do I stand behind my bike and begin a* Braveheart *speech to convince all these men that I am in fact one of them, and they should trust that the bike is not being stolen? Or should I hop on and race off as fast as I can?* I legit was scoping out the easiest path of escape when I heard the window bang open behind me.

"He's with us. Don't you boys worry!" Kathy to the rescue! I have never felt more relieved that an Amish woman had my back than I did in that moment right there. Come to think of it, that's the first time an Amish woman has ever had my back.

All at once, the men's heads tilted up almost in unison and their gazes left me.

I zipped off.

I had to do some self-talk on the ride home to keep myself from landing in a really bad place in my brain. *You would have assumed you were stealing the bike, too, if you'd been them. You keep an eye out for strange cars in your neighborhood, too, Carlos. You watch out for your neighbors too.*

By the time I got back to the farm, I was way too deep in my head about the whole thing. I rode straight to the Poppy House and parked my e-bike. I sat on the front steps and looked out at the little lambs playing in the pasture. I started thinking about all the things the Amish and I don't see eye to eye on. Which was *a lot.* And honestly, we hadn't talked about any of that because it wasn't the point of this little experiment. But that moment at the auction had definitely triggered me.

You know what I would have done had I been back at home with my phone? I would have numbed my mind. I would have escaped from the painful reality by ignoring it. But I didn't have that option now. So you know what I did instead? I did what I knew I needed to do but didn't want to do. I got up, got on my bike, and started pedaling back to the auction. I rode straight to the same bike rack I had been parked at before and, wouldn't you know it, the same Amish men that had been sitting there before were still sitting there when I got back.

I marched straight over to a group of three of them and introduced myself. "Hey, there. My name is Carlos Whittaker," I said. "I'm a friend of Willis and Kathy, and I want to apologize for speeding off without saying hello earlier."

"Why, hello there, Carlos," said one of the men. "My name is Marvin. I don't know Willis, but I know his brother. And we knew who you were earlier."

They knew who I was? Then why were they staring a hole through me?

"You guys didn't think I was stealing a bike?" I asked kind of jokingly, even though I was 100 percent serious.

"Oh, no sir. Not at all," Marvin said. "To be honest, we were just giggling at how you are kinda dressed like us, and you are wearing the straw hat like us, and well, you aren't Amish. So I guess you could say that you were just fun to look at. Sorry if we were staring!" he chuckled, and so did I. I mean, I guess I would have stared, too, if I were him.

We talked for an hour. Marvin was there with his son, who was selling some things at the flea market. Marvin told me he'd almost left the Amish before he got married but is glad he stayed. I ended up having the best convo with him. And I would have missed it if I'd had my phone. I would have numbed my brain with some scrolling and I definitely would not have gone back to meet Marvin. I would have labeled him with wrong assumptions and created a story that lived in my head for years to come. All because I was offended.

Now I need to add something here. Some things are worth getting offended about. It's not always wrong to feel offended. I just think the speed at which offense shows up in our lives could probably be cranked down a gear or two. The speed at which we go from not offended to offended has gotten so fast. And to be honest, it's not all our fault. We live in a world that is absolutely wired for outrage. And I am not using *wired* in a tongue-in-cheek way. Literally, the online world is wired for outrage. Headlines shout at us nonstop, social media feeds are boiling over with rage, and comment sections are dumpster fires we should avoid at all costs. It's enough to make even the most levelheaded, even-keeled human react in surprising ways.

So what can we do? How do we leave room for getting offended about things that are legitimately offensive while also lessening the ease with which we get offended? Try these on for a bit, and watch your blood pressure lower and your peace increase.

1. **RECOGNIZE THAT MOST TRIGGERING CONTENT IS CREATED TO BUILD AN AUDIENCE OR AN INCOME.** The majority of the most triggering content that I consume is made by accounts that get paid for my views. Legitimately. Most of the well-produced content out there that makes your blood boil is literally making money off your blood boiling. And suddenly you begin to see that much of the triggering content is a business built on rage. On both sides of most issues, a lot of people are making money on us being offended. Once I realized that, I began to lessen the amount of capital I put in that content. And I decided to unfollow and mute certain accounts. Your mental health is too important. You got this. Mute. Unfollow. Breathe . . .

2. **ASSUME THE BEST (MOST OF THE TIME).** Most people are not setting out with the intention of offending you. We have been conditioned to become offended every single time someone disagrees with us. But we must get back to the place where people disagreeing with us does not mean that they are against *us*. Back to the place where we understand that different experiences and different upbringings allow us to see things differently. There's no way I'll ever understand what it's like to look at topics from my buddy Brian's point of view. I'm not Brian. He's a white, middle-aged surfer from Laguna, California. I'm just not going to see things from his perspective. But I can allow myself to understand that his perspective is built off lived experience. And that alone can get us a long way.

3. **DON'T CONFUSE SOMEONE HAVING A DIFFERING OPIN-ION WITH SOMEONE ATTACKING.** Opinions are not the same as attacks. Not everything that we disagree with someone about is an attack on our values. Remember that opinions are subjective. Therefore, we need not be offended

by something subjective. Just because your cousin Lenny holds a differing belief on a hot-button issue does not mean he is questioning your entire existence. If we want to get back to not being offended by every single thing that *feels offensive* in the moment, we have to figure out how to separate opinion from personal attacks.

4. **NOT EVERY ARGUMENT IS WORTH HAVING, AND NOT EVERY COMMENT DESERVES A REBUTTAL.** I have to remind myself of this old adage a lot. I don't know who said it, but it has stuck with me: "Sometimes the best response is no response." It's true. The amount of times I've begun typing a long comment to rip someone's idea apart before literally deleting it and walking away is too many to count.

Not that I need to remind us here, but being less offended *does not mean* being more apathetic. It simply means that we are choosing where to best invest our energy and making sure that we are responding with *reason* and not with *rage*.

Willis had finished auctioning off his lambs, so we ended up going for a two-hour bike ride to eat some Troyer's bologna sandwiches at a small grocery store in a valley a few miles away. When I tell you that I hadn't had a bologna sandwich since fifth grade, I need you to believe me. And when I tell you I had three that day, I need you to believe that too. *The food.*

Willis and I had the best talk on our long ride home. We talked about things that we probably disagree on—hot-topic issues. And we talked about things we probably agree on.

"Willis, you know I spent a lot of 2020 teaching white people about the Black experience in America," I said about an hour into our bike ride home.

"Oh yes, I know. Christa told me all about your Instagram page," he said.

Oh crap. Homeboy has been snooping. What else does he know?

"Did you know that today I thought the men standing by the bikes thought I was stealing the e-bike? Then Kathy stuck her head out the window and told them I was good, but the whole thing bothered me, so I went back to talk with them. I kinda awkwardly asked if they thought I was stealing the bike, but they said no. They said they were just staring at me because I looked funny dressed like them even though I'm not Amish. It was a whole thing."

"Oh, they definitely thought you were stealing that bike," Willis said. "And they probably thought you looked funny too. We've had a rash of e-bike thefts at the auction, and everyone is sort of on edge and looking out for each other. They for sure thought you were stealing one."

I had to laugh.

I laughed because *of course they did*, and because I was having a conversation with an Amish man through Bluetooth helmets while riding the back roads of Holmes County, Ohio.

What was my life?

And what was I going to bring back to my real life?

I did know one thing. When I get offended, instead of picking up my phone, I'm going to pick up a conversation with whoever has offended me. Even if they lie when they tell me I'm wrong.

CHAPTER 20

DO NOT DISTURB

When I tell you that I was living my wife's dream, I mean that I couldn't believe it was me rather than her who was getting to do this. The first ten years of our marriage, she read Amish romance novels every night before bed. She loved the simple way of life. She loved moving at God speed. To this day, if she could throw her phone into the deepest ocean and never see it again, she would. We used to joke and say, "Heather is *almost* Amish."

At one point Heather discovered a small Amish community about ninety minutes south of our home in Nashville. She would take the kids there every so often to visit with people living such a different life, buy milk and eggs, and shop for furniture. Over a period of years she really hit it off with an Amish man named Danny. He was sort of the patriarch of the community. And having lived in Mount Hope for two weeks, I can 100 percent tell you that this was not the same order of Amish I had lived with. The Amish in Ethridge, Tennessee, were definitely among the most conservative and primitive Amish. There wasn't a lot to their simple lives. When Heather once asked Danny to write her a letter every day for a week so she could see what sort of things he did, he agreed. The first letter was fascinating. He wrote in the most beautiful cursive and kept almost a running journal of every hour.

5:30 a.m.: Milk the cows.
6:30 a.m.: Start working in the woodshed.
7:30 a.m.: Breakfast.
8:30 a.m.: Check on the horses in the south pasture.
9:00 a.m.: Set out for-sale items in the yard booth.

And so on.

It was super detailed. And then when she opened the second letter to read what he'd written about the next day—and this is no joke—it looked like he had put the first letter on a copy machine and sent her the exact same thing. Except you could tell that he'd rewritten it. He just didn't change a thing. He sent six more letters that were *verbatim* what he had written in the first letter. We laughed and laughed at how cute it was that he didn't just write it once and say, "This is it. Every day." But Heather had asked for seven days of letters, and he wrote them. The Amish are people of their word. When they say they are going to do something, they do it.

On one of my last few days in Mount Hope, I went to church with one of Willis and Kathy's neighbors. Everyone called him Junior, and he had also become a good friend. I went to *Amish* church. In that single four-hour church service I attempted to greet a man with a holy kiss (only to get rejected as I leaned in), sat on a pew next to Amish men while all the ladies sat in pews across the room, sang hymns that were as hauntingly beautiful as they were slow, listened to two sermons in Pennsylvania Dutch that touched my heart even though I couldn't understand the language being spoken, and had an amazing after-church meal with the entire congregation. I felt more welcomed into the community than ever. I really loved these people. They were so, so kind.

I had also spent the last two weeks shearing sheep (if a sheep were to walk in my front door right now, I could shear that thing in fifteen minutes flat), going to softball games (did you know that Amish women play softball in their dresses and can rip a softball in half they swing so hard?), and—of course—having hours and hours of heartfelt, deep conversations.

I hadn't been ready for most of that, but you know what I was ready for? I was ready to go home—to bring everything I'd learned back to my regular life. Or I could even say I was ready to bring everything I'd lived back to my regular life. Because that is the truth of what happened. I'd lived. I'd truly lived. I had fallen in love with this Amish family. Who knew that spending weeks with people that were nothing like me would impact me in such a powerful way? I know it's said that you must never judge a book by its cover. And I agree with that more than ever. I had gotten deep into the book of the Amish. I had witnessed them including me in things that I never could have dreamed I would be included in.

The Amish quickly went from a subculture I was fascinated by to people who ministered to me. Turns out they are just like you and me. They have dreams. Hopes. Desires. And by including me, they gave *me* some new hopes, dreams, and desires. I had learned to squeeze every last drop of life out of every single conversation. I'm just so very grateful that I was accepted and folded into their community so effortlessly.

Heather flew out so she could join me for my last forty-eight hours with the Amish—and honestly, I didn't think she was going to want to come home.

But I was ready. *Let's go.*

I spent the last three weeks of my seven-week, screen-free experiment at home with my family. I was still unplugged, but life didn't feel "unplugged" because unplugged now felt normal. It just felt *right*. I was still praying five times a day, monk-style. And I was using my Amish handyman skills to fix every single thing Heather had decided needing fixing around the house. The honey-do list was a mile long, and with all the work ethic of WilLos, I finished in two days flat what previously would have been a five-week ordeal. Heather kept saying over and over, "I love Amish Carlos!"[i]

During my three screen-free weeks with my family, we went to Yellowstone and I spent the entire trip in deeper conversations with the kids than I'd had in years. So much had happened that not a single person on the internet knew about! What a novel idea. But I will tell you that I was stalked by a bear on the banks of the Madison River and had no phone to document it, so I had to ask the person screaming "BEAR! BEAR!" at me from the other side of the road if they would email me their video. That was so analog of me.

I went on dates with Heather back home in Nashville, and not once was I tempted to look at my phone on the date—because it wasn't there. I went on walks in my neighborhood without listening to podcasts or listening to music and instead just listened to the world around me.

I was a different man. All because I didn't have a phone.

I had been looking forward to everything about being back home except one: I didn't want to get back on my phone. I mean, why would I? I had just experienced life for seven weeks as it was actually *supposed* to be experienced. It's hard to adequately describe the level of fear I had about getting back on my phone and what

i. Around the end of my three weeks unplugged at home, I walked into the bathroom and saw myself in the mirror. "*Whoa*, Mountain Man." I hadn't shaved since I'd arrived at the abbey, and I was looking about as Amish as I could possibly look.

202

was waiting for me. Especially the number of texts and emails that would be clamoring for a response. As the day grew closer for this little experiment to end, I told Heather I didn't think I could do it. I didn't think I could go back to living the way I had before—to being who I'd been before.

"Carlos, we had this exact conversation weeks ago when you were at the monastery," she said. "Remember? You called me saying you wanted to quit. And now we're having the same conversation, but backward. You don't have to go back to the way things were before. You know what you want now. So go and get it."

Go and get it. I knew what she meant. She meant that I needed to do two things. First I needed to go and get my brain rescanned, which can I tell you, I was really nervous about. Of all the things I was feeling worried about, for some reason I was really focusing on whether this experiment had had any measurable effect on my brain, or if all the benefits I thought I was experiencing were just a placebo effect. I was also concerned about not getting sucked back into my old phone patterns. I mean, while part of me couldn't imagine letting that happen, the reality is that I do love social media and telling stories on the internet. Would it be possible for me to reengage with screens while still holding on to everything I'd learned and all the transformations I'd experienced?

All I knew for sure was that I needed to finish strong. And it was time to bring this screen-free experiment to a close.

———

The plan was to fly to Los Angeles, where I would stop by my best friend Brian's house to pick up my phone before heading to Dr. Amen's office for the follow-up brain scan. Remember Brian, the friend who'd taken my phone from me and dropped me off at the monastery? He had my phone this entire time. Brian was out of town and wouldn't be getting home until later that evening. So he made sure I had access to his home and told me he'd leave my phone sitting on his office desk.

After landing, I got in my rental car and headed to Laguna. I had to navigate from memory—which, may I add, was pretty good after all those weeks without GPS! Never even made one wrong turn.

When I arrived at Brian's neighborhood I legitimately got nauseous. And I began to panic a little. I was really, really scared. I didn't know exactly what I was scared of in the moment, but looking back I can tell you it was the unknown. It was the exact same fear that I had at the beginning of this little experiment—only backwards, as Heather so perfectly summed up. I was fearful that I wouldn't be as present with my family. I was scared that Heather would be disappointed after getting the screen-free version of me for the past three weeks. Despite all the good things that my phone (and screens in general) had brought into my life over the years, the damage it had caused and the potential for future harm was looming large. I knew that the solution wasn't just to walk away from screens forever, turning this temporary experiment into my permanent new way of life. But man, was it hard to imagine picking up that phone again.

I pulled into Brian's driveway and got out. I had just my backpack, 'cause it was just an overnight trip. I unlocked the front door and walked upstairs to his office. When I opened the door, there it was. Exactly where he said it would be. Face up and unplugged. I walked over and picked it up. I wondered if just holding it was going to skew my brain scan.

I was a mess.

I walked back to the car and made my way to Dr. Amen's clinic. This time I did get lost. But I figured it out. I pulled into the parking lot. Turned the car off. Took a deep breath. Walked into the office and took the elevator up to Dr. Amen's floor. They were waiting for me.

"Hello, Carlos!" Jeff said. Jeff was Dr. Amen's head of communications and media. They were also going to document the day because this whole screen-free experiment intrigued Dr. Amen and his team as much as it did me.

The brain scan was just as terrible as the first time. I did all the same tests. And let it be known, the lab technician was even the same one as before. It was so surreal to see him again. His presence still made me nervous with anticipation, but this time for a slightly different reason. I was less concerned with all of the buzzing and beeping and strapping my head to the board I was lying down on, and more worried that my brain wouldn't look any different.

"How was it with no phone? Have you turned it back on yet?" he asked.

"Not yet. I didn't want you to waste your time with this scan by melting my brain all over again a few minutes before walking in here!" The lab tech laughed politely at my attempted joke.

This time it felt like the brain scan lasted even longer. I was recording the entire procedure with my old-school, screen-free Sony camera—the one I'd been documenting my journey with over the last seven weeks. I don't know why I decided to record the entire scan, because I realized two minutes in that the video was just going to be me lying completely still for thirty minutes. Riveting content.[ii]

Finally, the scan was over. After all of the waiting, all of the praying, all of the chanting, all of the farming, all of the beholding. The time had come for Dr. Amen to tell me if my brain was any different.

---

ii. Until I watched the footage a few weeks later and realized that my fly was down the entire time I was getting scanned. Like, wide open. So nope, that footage will never make the light of day.

"Carlos! How was it?" he asked as he walked into the office and took a seat across from me.

"Oh, Dr. Amen, do you have a few weeks to help me unpack it all? It was incredible."

"Well, I don't have a few weeks, but what I do have are your brain scans. Do you think your brain looks different?" he asked.

I remember almost not wanting him to tell me. I *felt* so different now that I didn't want some brain scan to tell me I wasn't, which would mess up how good I was feeling. I didn't want him to tell me that my brain looked worse. I didn't want him to tell me that my brain looked the same. I felt like a completely different person, so I didn't want him to show me anything on a scan that might contradict that.

"Gosh, I don't know. I honestly don't know. I just wanted to see what—I don't know—if it was technology or stress, not knowing the news. But I know that my anxiety is lower. But I don't know if that's a physical body thing or a brain thing. I don't know. So I guess go ahead and tell me," I said, just like the Enneagram Nine peacemaker and recovering people-pleaser that I am.

"Well, it does," he said, smiling. "There's a difference. The thing that had me sort of concerned was this asymmetrical cerebellum. So this is—I almost think of this as like this central processing part of the brain. And on the right side it's busy, but on the left side it's slow. See how much better it is? I mean, it's a very marked difference.

"Your emotional centers are actually up, and it's sort of a big difference. And so with meditation we often see an activation, and the right lateral temporal lobe is often called the 'God spot,' so maybe you're more in touch with it. But there's clearly a change. When we look at the outside surface, not so much. If we look back here, see this dent? That seems better. But the thing that I'm really impressed with is the cerebellar change."

"The cerebellar..." I repeated. "Can you tell me more about that?"

"So it's really important," Dr. Amen explained. "I have to call it the Rodney Dangerfield part of the brain because it gets no respect. Anyway, it has half the brain's neurons. So 50 percent. Your brain has 100 billion neurons. Fifty percent of them are in your cerebellum. It's involved in motor coordination but also thought coordination—how quickly you can integrate new information. And we know it's also about emotion, cognition, behavior, and automatic processing. So meditation and prayer—it activates it. And physical expertise activates it. So it looks like we've got some bigger action in the cerebellum. Your cingulate is much busier, that's right here. I think of it as the brain's gear shifter. It allows you to go from thought to thought, move you from idea to idea, be flexible, go with the flow.

"Now, we know this was an anecdotal experiment, so we don't know what it was that made the biggest difference. If it was your time at the abbey with the twenty-three hours a day of silence and the prayers five times a day. Or if it was working hard on the farm and also riding your bike for miles every day. But we know your brain changed. And I know I'm a neurologist, but I don't have to look at your brain to see the change in you. You just seem lighter. Congrats, my friend. You did a really hard thing."

I could legit feel my lungs breathe deeper at the exact moment he finished those sentences. I *knew* things were different in my brain. I was just scared that we wouldn't be able to see or measure the difference. I could feel my smile. Dr. Amen went on for about fifteen more minutes, showing me things that were different and what else I could do to continue this healing trend. I was just beaming on his sofa the entire time.

"Here's my number," Dr. Amen said, handing me a piece of paper with his cell phone number on it. "Text me if you need anything." He paused briefly, smiled, and then said, "Um, wait a second. Do you even text anymore?"

"Well, not for another few minutes. I'm about to go turn my phone back on!" I replied.

I gave him a hug and left his office.

Now I was about to do the most terrifying thing I had done in seven weeks.

Turn my phone back on.

I went down to the courtyard outside Dr. Amen's office building, put my backpack on a table, pulled out my phone, and just stared at it. The black screen stared back at me, begging me to turn it on. I walked away. I walked in circles around the table several times before finally sitting down. But I couldn't do it. So I stood back up and walked around the table a few more times.

I must have looked crazy to anyone walking by or watching me from the offices above. Like maybe I was doing some kind of ritual around my backpack. I wondered if the security guards might already be on their way.

I took out a charging cable, plugged it into my external battery, plugged the other end into my phone, and held my breath for what felt like two minutes until the white Apple logo finally popped up.

Then I put the phone back down. Facedown on the table. I needed to remember to breathe.

If all of this sounds a little dramatic, you have to remember that not only had I not received one single notification for nearly two months, I also didn't know what was happening on planet Earth. I didn't know the news. I didn't know anything. So I knew there would be *a lot* waiting for me when I picked it up.

Suddenly, there was a chorus of notifications. *Ding! Ding! Ding! Ding! Ding!*

There were 1,492 text messages waiting for me. Literally.

Want to know what I did?

Select *all*. *Delete*.

I didn't even hesitate.

So sorry if one of those texts was from you and you are reading this right now.

I opened up Instagram and posted a photo I'd taken with my Sony camera of me holding my phone upside-down and perpendicular to my ear, as if I no longer knew how to use it. And then I jumped back in headfirst.

———

So what changed in my life because of this experiment?

Oh, my friend. Let me tell you.

First of all, I walk a lot more, and I walk slowly. I think of my monk friends all the time and try to match my pace with theirs.

I notice things more because I have practiced noticing. Like, I purposely try to notice something nice about anyone I'm talking to. I notice shifts in the wind. I notice when my wife gets a haircut! That was new.

I don't immediately look up answers to questions I have.

I don't ever walk and look at my phone at the same time. Those are now separate.

I spend *a lot* of time in silence, including on car rides or on walks. I no longer fill those activities with listening to audiobooks or podcasts.

I try and stand in *awe* of God as much as I can by reading his Word on a daily basis and by not just letting my phone be the thing that teaches me about him. I go look for him in the mountains and deserts and the world around us that dwarfs any cathedral we could ever build. I just spend a lot more time looking for him.

I look for *behold* moments daily. For example, when my dad, whose dementia is progressing, recognizes me when I walk in the house again, I *behold*.

I savor like a freaking savor gold medalist. Coffee in a ceramic mug *forever*.

I don't use my phone as an alarm clock in my bedroom anymore. In fact, I don't allow my phone in there at all.

I try to spend at least thirty minutes at every single meal. Never under twenty.

I turn *off* Siri when I drive.

I check the dew on my boots every morning.

I look you in the eye when you talk to me and I never, ever, look through you.

And I'm sure I do a lot of other things because of the incredible weeks I spent rediscovering the art of being human.

Here's another thing I think is important for you to know. I'm now back on my phone five and a half hours a day, which means I shaved off about ninety minutes from my previous average. I'm not a hero. There are days I fail and go back to the addiction of seven or eight hours in a day. But now I simply know that there is another way of life, one that tastes better and nourishes me. I now desire that more than the junk food of being on my phone all the time. See, that is the problem. We have forgotten what tastes better, what nourishes us. And I hope that my experiment reminded you of the flavor of life you have been missing.

We aren't ever going to lose these screens.

But we can gain our lives back while living with these screens.

There is so much life waiting for you to live, right on the other side of Do Not Disturb.

ACKNOWLEDGMENTS

Every night of our marriage after crawling into bed, my wife, Heather, opens up an Amish romance novel and reads a few pages before peacefully drifting to sleep. I don't know how many of those books exist, but after twenty-four years she still hasn't gotten to the last one. And Heather, look at you now—you are living in your own novel. Thank you for taking care of literally every single thing in our lives and the kids' lives while I was away shearing sheep and saving hummingbirds. I know this was your dream that I got to live out. If this book sells a lot, I'll buy you a farm in Ohio near the Millers.

To Sohaila, Seanna, and Losiah: You actually blow me away at how you live out so many of the principles in this book. I'm sorry it took your dad moving in with monks for him to realize there is more life to be lived on the other side of my phone screen (even though you're probably annoyed at how much eye contact I make with you now).

Mom and Dad: I'm so grateful that you modeled what it looks like to live a curious life. It's because of you that so many are impacted. I love you.

To Kelli, Jami, Lani, and Hayley, my KCH Management fam: This project would not be what it is without your dedication to my vision and the support you have given me. I'm so grateful to have found you when I did. The next twenty-five books are going to be a blast!

To Whitney from Wisconsin: I actually laugh when anyone calls you my assistant because you literally are so much more. Your eyes, mind, and heart have helped shape this book into what it is. Thank you for saying yes to working with the Whittakers. We are so grateful for all you are.

To Alexander Field: I know you thought this book idea was crazy when I first sent you the idea, but just wait till you see the next idea. You have championed all my ideas since you became my agent, and I'm so grateful for you.

To Daniel, Andrew, and the entire team over at Nelson: *we did it*! You turned this crazy idea into an actual book. I'm so grateful to be on this journey with all of you.

And to the Instafamilia: Now you know where I disappeared to two years ago. Thank you for not unfollowing me when you thought I went to prison. Wait, Alex, I have an idea . . .

NOTES

INTRODUCTION

1. Laura Tenenbaum, "Digging in the Dirt Really Does Make People Happier," *Forbes*, January 29, 2020, https://www.forbes.com/sites/lauratenenbaum/2020/01/29/digging-in-the-dirt-really-does-make-people-happier/?sh=26e6bd6031e1.

CHAPTER 5: WONDER

1. Dictionary.com, s.v. "wonder (*v.*)," accessed November 27, 2023, https://www.dictionary.com/browse/wonder.
2. Saint Jerome, "Letter 22," in *Letters of Saint Jerome*, Nicene and Post-Nicene Fathers, 2nd series, ed. Philip Schaff and Henry Wave, trans. W. H. Fremantle, G. Lewis, and W. G. Martley (Buffalo, NY: Christian Literature Publishing Co., 1893), 37, archived at New Advent, https://www.newadvent.org/fathers/3001022.htm.

CHAPTER 6: BEING

1. "Oblates," Sisters of the Order of St. Benedict, accessed February 29, 2024, https://sbm.osb.org/partnership/oblates/.

NOTES

CHAPTER 7: SOLITUDE

1. Blaise Pascal, *Pascal's Pensées* (New York: E. P. Dutton and Co., 1958), 139, archived at Project Gutenberg, https://www.gutenberg.org/files/18269/18269-h/18269-h.htm.
2. Kristi Baerg MacDonald, "Loneliness Unlocked: Associations with Smartphone Use and Personality," *Acta Psychologica* 221 (November 2021): 103454, https://doi.org/10.1016/j.actpsy.2021.103454; Anthony Silard, "Is Your Phone Making You Lonelier?," *Psychology Today*, September 8, 2020, https://www.psychologytoday.com/us/blog/the-art-living-free/202009/is-your-phone-making-you-lonelier.

CHAPTER 8: BEHOLDING

1. Quoted in John Behr, "The Glory of God," in *Irenaeus of Lyons: Identifying Christianity* (Oxford, UK: Oxford University Press, 2013), 121, https://doi.org/10.1093/acprof:oso/9780199214624.003.0004.

CHAPTER 11: BORED

1. Drake Baer, "Why Your iPhone Addiction Is Snuffing Out Your Creativity," *Fast Company*, April 10, 2013, https://www.fastcompany.com/3008060/why-your-iphone-addiction-snuffing-your-creativity.

CHAPTER 12: SAVOR

1. Tasha Strawszewski and Jason T. Siegel, "Positive Emotion Infusions: Can Savoring Increase Help-Seeking Intentions Among People with Depression?," *Applied Psychology: Health and Well-Being* 10, no. 1 (March 2018): 171–90, https://doi.org/10.1111/aphw.12122.

CHAPTER 15: THE TABLE

1. Carlos Whittaker and Dan Allender, "Episode 114: Mental Health Series—Healing Our Trauma with Dan Allender," July 22, 2023, in *The Carlos Whittaker Podcast*, produced by Carlos Whittaker, podcast, MP3 audio, 53:23, https://www.carloswhittaker.com/podcast/episode-114-mental-health-series-healing-our-trauma-with-dan-allender.
2. Kathleen M. Zelman, "Slow Down, You Eat Too Fast," WebMD,

214

accessed March 5, 2024, https://www.webmd.com/obesity/features
/slow-down-you-eat-too-fast.

3. "Fact Check: Are American Families Really Not Eating Dinner
Together Anymore?," Fontana, accessed February 29, 2024, https://
www.fontanaforniusa.com/blogs/news-1/fact-check-are-american
-families-really-not-eating-dinner-together-anymore.

4. "New Survey: 91% of Parents Say Their Family Is Less Stressed When
They Eat Together," American Heart Association, October 10, 2022,
https://newsroom.heart.org/news/new-survey-91-of-parents-say
-their-family-is-less-stressed-when-they-eat-together.

5. Linda S. Pagani et al., "Early School-Age Family Meal Characteristics
Matter for the Later Development of Boys and Girls," *Dialogues in
Health* 1 (December 2022): 100007, https://doi.org/10.1016/j.dialog
.2022.100007.

CHAPTER 16: GET LOST

1. John Silcox, "Get Lost—It Could Be Good for You," *Audi*, 39,
archived at John C. Silcox (website), accessed May 1, 2024,
https://www.johncsilcox.com/get-lost-could-be-good-for-you.

ABOUT THE AUTHOR

Carlos Whittaker is a bestselling author and expert storyteller who uses his vast and varied life experiences to captivate and engage audiences. In his books—*How to Human, Enter Wild, Moment Maker,* and *Kill the Spider*—he reminds us that when we are connected to God and good to ourselves, we can be even better for others. Join Carlos and countless others in the pursuit of being human together. He and his wife, Heather, live with their three amazing children in Nashville, Tennessee, where you can find them working on the family farm and planning trips around the world.

NOTES

_____

_____

_____

_____

_____

_____

_____

_____

_____

_____

_____

_____

NOTES

NOTES

NOTES

NOTES

NOTES

_____

_____

_____

_____

_____

_____

_____

_____

_____

_____

_____

_____

_____